Emotion Hacked

How Technology Steals
Your Feelings, Thoughts, and Memories

About the Author. Serene Kim

Serene Kim is a writer who seeks to understand life more deeply. She asks thoughtful questions about the world, humanity, and herself, interpreting them with care. Her writing offers clarity and direction. Rooted in personal experience, her inquiries extend into history, politics, economics, culture, and beyond. Through her work, she inspires readers to see differently and to speak with a voice uniquely their own.

Table of Contents

Prologue.

Can Emotions Really Be Hacked?

When people first hear the phrase, "Emotions can be hacked," they often react with skepticism. "Seriously? Even emotions can be manipulated?" "Hacking feelings? That sounds like a conspiracy theory." And that's understandable. For as long as we can remember, emotions have been seen as something deeply personal—an inarticulable essence of being human. But today, the world is telling a very different story. Across the globe, recognition is rising.

- The European Union has classified emotional data as sensitive information under GDPR, making it illegal to collect or analyze it without explicit consent.
- The U.S. Senate has proposed legislation labeling emotion-based behavioral manipulation as both a privacy violation and a threat to democracy.
- The United Nations has declared emotions, memories, and beliefs essential parts of inner identity, safeguarding them against technological intrusion.
- Canada has categorized emotion recognition AI as a high-risk technology.
- Germany has moved to enshrine mental autonomy as a constitutional right, seeking to regulate emotionally manipulative political advertising.

The world already acknowledges it: emotional infringement is real.

Emotion Hacked begins with a single, urgent question: "The emotion I am feeling right now—is it truly mine?" For a long time, we believed emotions were the last fortress of freedom, the purest expression of the self. No one could touch them. No machine could measure them. They were ours alone.

But somewhere along the way, technology crept in—quietly, invisibly. Neuroscience revealed that the human brain operates through electrical signals. BCI (Brain-Computer Interface) technologies evolved to read and interpret these signals. Without even implanting a chip, machines can now infer emotional states from subtle clues: facial expressions, eye movements, brainwave patterns, voice tremors. Emotions have become measurable. Quantifiable. Predictable.

You probably didn't notice it. But your emotions have already been quietly, almost imperceptibly, nudged. When you scroll through a news feed, when your hand lingers on a headline, when an ad feels oddly well-timed, when a single video shifts your mood for the entire day— "I just felt off today." "Nothing special happened, but I felt so restless." "I bought it on impulse... Why did I do that?" You brush it off. But perhaps your emotional stream had already been gently, expertly guided—long before you realized it.

The machine had already read: the colors you gravitate toward, the words that pierce you, the microseconds of hesitation, the unconscious flinch at a certain sound.

And quietly, it stirred small waves in your emotional sea. A ripple today. A tide tomorrow. A reshaped memory. A different decision.

Emotions flow. Memories stack upon those currents. And our lives are built atop those memories. If emotions can be designed, can memories be engineered too? And if memories can be rewritten— Whose life are we truly living? Whose choices are we really making?

This book traces that silent, dangerous flow: how technology reads emotions, how it induces emotional drift, how memories and judgments are subtly reconstructed, and how the very boundaries of human identity are being blurred.

Emotion Hacked proclaims: Technology has now reached the deepest layers of humanity. If so, the language to defend humanity must reach just as deep. Emotions are not data. Emotions are human.

The question is no longer personal. It is the collective question of our era: "Are your emotions still truly yours?"

Part 1.
When Brains and Computers Merge

Chapter 1. Why Elon Musk Put Chips in Human Brains

The Day a Worm's Brain Was Uploaded into a Robot

In the early 1970s, at the MRC Laboratory of Molecular Biology in Cambridge, England, a quiet revolution began. Sydney Brenner, a visionary scientist, posed a simple yet profound question: "If we could fully map the nervous system of the simplest organism, could we unlock the fundamental blueprint of life itself?" The subject of this experiment was the tiny worm Caenorhabditis elegans, barely visible to the human eye, with just 302 neurons. Yet, despite its simplicity, this worm demonstrated complex behaviors—it moved toward food, reacted to stimuli, and adapted to its environment.

Brenner and his team embarked on a groundbreaking experiment. Using electron microscopes, they meticulously sliced the worm into thousands of thin sections and photographed each slice. Then, they manually traced the connections of each neuron across the countless images. The laboratory tables were soon covered with photos and hand-drawn lines. This process took years, from the 1970s into the 1980s, but in 1986, the team completed the world's first "connectome"—a complete map of all 302 neurons and their approximately 7,000 synaptic connections. For this monumental achievement, Brenner was awarded the Nobel Prize in Physiology or Medicine in 2002. This effort wasn't just about dissecting a worm; it was the first scientific proof that life, consciousness, and behavior could be reduced to electrical signals and patterns of connection. Fast forward to 2014, another breakthrough: researchers successfully converted the C. elegans connectome into digital code and implanted it into a simple robot equipped with just two wheels and an ultrasonic sensor. This wasn't the work of a large institution, but rather an open-source collaboration between scientists, engineers, and developers worldwide. Their question was simple: "Can we recreate life through code?" The result was the OpenWorm project. Without any programmed commands, the robot began to move on its own, avoiding obstacles, responding to light and collisions, and even appearing to act with "intention." Scientists declared: "Life is not just a collection of cells. It is patterns, connections, and electrical signals." For the first time, it was proven that machines could read and replicate these signals through code.

Elon Musk's Neuralink: Implanting Chips into Human Brains

But the worm was just the beginning. If we could digitize 302 neurons, what about the billions of neurons in the human brain? One man took on this challenge: Elon Musk. In 2016, he founded Neuralink, aiming to create an interface that links human brains directly to artificial intelligence, ensuring humanity's survival in a future where AI might surpass us.

In 2021, Neuralink showcased a stunning demonstration: a monkey playing a video game using only its mind. Initially, the monkey controlled the game using a joystick while

Neuralink's chip recorded the brain activity patterns related to moving the joystick. Over time, the chip learned to interpret these neural signals, mapping the command "I want to move left" or "move right" into actions.

Then, the joystick was removed. Miraculously, the monkey continued to play the game, controlling it purely through thought. No hands, no buttons, just brain signals interpreted by the Neuralink chip. This moment was a revelation: "You can control machines with your mind."

Neuralink then achieved another major milestone: the successful brain-computer interface implant in a human brain. The recipient, Noland Arbaugh, a 29-year-old who had been paralyzed from a tragic accident, had a fully active mind despite his immobile body. Neuralink aimed to tap into that potential. The Link chip, about the size of a coin (23mm in diameter), housed over 1,000 hair-thin electrodes, which were carefully placed in the brain's motor cortex. These electrodes detected faint electrical signals, translating them into computer commands via AI algorithms.

At first, the chip simply observed and recorded the signals generated by different thoughts. But soon, Arbaugh was able to control a computer cursor with just his mind. Without moving a finger or speaking a word, he could mentally command "left," "right," or "click," and the cursor responded naturally.

This breakthrough opened the door to a new era: an era where thought alone could move the digital world. Even more astonishing, Arbaugh was able to control a robotic arm. By simply thinking "grab" or "move," his motor neurons fired, and the robotic arm responded.

Neuralink's ambitions went far beyond reading thoughts. Research was underway to regulate emotions, guide decision-making, and even stimulate memories. Imagine being able to activate dormant pleasure circuits in the brain to treat depression—not just improving mood but fundamentally altering emotional states. All of this would happen invisibly, without external wires or visible changes. The Link chip operates quietly inside the skull, and from the outside, everything appears normal. Yet, inside, profound shifts may be taking place—raising unsettling questions about whether the emotions we feel are truly our own.

Neuralink's ultimate vision includes backing up memories, modifying emotions, and allowing external devices to compute on behalf of the human brain. Musk envisions a future where memories can be stored, downloaded, and recalled. In this new reality, memories are no longer fleeting fragments of the past. They can be digitized, stored like computer files, retrieved at will—and even edited. Forgotten memories could be sharpened, unwanted memories erased, and entirely new memories implanted. Musk describes memory backup as "a path to expanding human consciousness." If realized, this technology would not only read brainwaves but would manage the very flow of identity itself. A world where humans become part of machines, and machines design human consciousness, is no longer science fiction—it is the reality unfolding before us.

Chapter 2. How Do Thoughts Reach Machines?

Thoughts Are Electricity Signals

We experience our thoughts as a flowing stream—images, emotions, decisions rising in our minds. But scientifically, thoughts are nothing more than electrical signals. The human brain is a vast electrical network, made up of billions of neurons, each exchanging tiny electrical currents. Right now, tens of millions of these electrical exchanges are flashing through our brains like lightning—when we rejoice, doubt, love, or regret. Every moment is simply a flow of electrical impulses between neurons. Thoughts are not passion or logic. Thoughts are faster than light, pure electrical movement.

These signals don't stay locked inside our brains. They leak out as electromagnetic waves called brainwaves. Without speaking or moving, we are constantly broadcasting the "now" of ourselves into the world. These signals are so faint that we often go through life unaware of them. But now, technology can listen. Machines have begun to hear the silent whispers of our brains.

Brain-Computer Interface (BCI)

Enter Brain-Computer Interface technology—BCI. BCI reads brainwaves, deciphers them, and can even send signals back to the brain. A bridge between thoughts and machines is being built.

The brain produces five primary types of brainwaves:

- Delta (0.5–4 Hz): Deep sleep, unconsciousness — a body in complete shutdown
- Theta (4–8 Hz): Dreaming, imagination, emotional turbulence — unstable creativity
- Alpha (8–12 Hz): Relaxation, calm, meditation — a mind opening up
- Beta (12–30 Hz): Focus, judgment, alertness — the center of decision-making

- Gamma (30+ Hz): Fear, crisis, excitement, full immersion — emotional explosions

Each wave quietly reveals our emotional and mental states. BCI technology reads these waves and analyzes how focused, stressed, fatigued, or emotionally unstable a person might be. Even without words or movements, our brainwaves silently speak to the world.

We already live in the age of BCI. It is closer than most realize. Games where your character moves faster as your concentration deepens. Marketing studies that analyze brainwave reactions to advertisements. Study apps that visualize students' attention levels in real time. BCI has moved from laboratories into our daily lives. While we remain unaware, machines are quietly reading the rhythm of our thoughts and capturing the smallest tremors of emotion.

And BCI is no longer one-way. Initially, BCIs only read brain signals. Now, they can act first—gently nudging emotions, subtly guiding choices, and quietly shifting patterns of judgment. Military and civilian labs across the U.S., China, and Europe are already conducting experiments on emotional stimulation and decision-making manipulation.

BCI no longer asks, "Is it possible?" It demands a new question: "Who is using this technology, and for what purpose?"

BCI can be a technology that helps humanity. But it is also a technology that can quietly disturb the deepest freedoms of human existence—our emotions, memories, and judgments. This book stands at that boundary and asks: "Are these thoughts truly mine?"

Implanting Chips vs. Reading Signals from the Skin

BCI technology reaches the brain through two approaches:

- Invasive BCI (Implantable)
- Non-Invasive BCI (Surface-Level)

Invasive BCIs involve surgically opening the skull and implanting electrodes or chips directly into the brain. Since the sensors are placed next to neurons, signal detection is highly precise, sensitive, and responsive, with minimal noise. Subtle emotional changes can be captured as electrical patterns. However, the risks are significant: surgery, infection, bleeding, and the unsettling feeling of having "a machine inside my head." Invasive BCI is not just a technical issue—it questions the very boundary between human identity and technology.

Non-invasive BCIs don't enter the body. Instead, they use EEG sensors placed on the scalp, wearable headsets, or even remote wireless signals to detect brainwaves. No surgery. No pain. These BCIs are much more accessible, lower-cost, and easier for the public to experience. Consumer brainwave headsets, emotion-analysis devices, and eye-tracking systems are all part of this field.

But non-invasive BCIs come with hidden risks. Signals weaken as they pass through the skull and skin, making them more prone to noise and reducing precision. Most importantly, brainwaves can be read and emotions subtly influenced without the user's awareness. Hidden sensing, silent shaping—this is the double-edged sword of non-invasive BCI.

Despite these risks, non-invasive BCI is the fastest-commercializing and most widespread form of the technology. It quietly blends into everyday life—reading our emotions and behaviors through games, education, advertising, and healthcare. It is no longer a distant research tool. It is already shaping our consciousness, whether we notice it or not.

Chapter 3. When Machines Start Talking to Our Brains

The Brain and Machines Are Now in Dialogue

In the previous chapters, we explored how thoughts are electrical signals and how BCI technology is already capable of reading them. But the story doesn't end there. The bigger question is: where is this technology heading? It no longer stops at reading human thoughts—machines have begun talking back.

BCI technology is evolving along two distinct paths:

- Output BCI: Sending thoughts to machines.
- Input BCI: Machines sending signals into the brain.

At a glance, these seem simple. But the difference between the two could fundamentally reshape human existence.

Today, it's no longer enough to speak of "freedom to express thoughts"; we must also defend "freedom to protect our thoughts."

Output BCI: Technology That Sends Thoughts Out

Output BCI enables users to "send" their thoughts into the external world. When I think "move right," that thought becomes a brainwave, which is translated into a command that moves a wheelchair or robotic arm.

Thought → Signal → Machine Response.

Output BCI creates a direct bridge between willpower and the world.

EEG: Controlling Devices with Brainwaves

Electroencephalography (EEG) is the most common method for output BCIs. Headsets with sensors capture tiny electrical signals emitted from the scalp, interpreting them in real time.

A pioneer in this field is Emotiv, a U.S. neurotechnology startup. Their non-invasive BCI headsets allow users to control devices simply by wearing a lightweight headset—no surgery, no implants. Thoughts become commands, and those commands trigger real-world actions.

At first, the technology seemed magical. Without uttering a word or lifting a finger, users could think "launch the drone," and the drone would lift off.

Not just drones—users can steer game characters, change light colors, adjust music volume, or control smart home devices. Commands like "move left," "lower the volume," "open the door" come straight from thought.

Emotiv's technology is expanding into assistive devices for people with disabilities, psychological monitoring tools, and game controllers. Their headsets can now even read emotional states like stress, relaxation, or concentration, adjusting device behavior accordingly.

Once an expensive lab technology, BCI devices are now available commercially, costing just a few hundred dollars, with mobile app support.

But Emotiv's rise also raises unsettling questions: "If I can control machines with my mind, could someone else control my thoughts?"

Emotiv built the world's first mass-market BCI platform, turning thought into command—and their technology continues to evolve quietly.

ECoG: Reading Speech Directly from the Brain

While EEG reads brainwaves externally, Electrocorticography (ECoG) places electrodes directly on the brain's surface. This semi-invasive method captures brain signals with much higher precision.

Scientists recently achieved something remarkable: helping an ALS patient who had lost the ability to speak regain communication—through thought alone.

The patient had electrodes implanted over the motor speech areas of the brain. As she silently thought words like "water" or "thank you," each thought generated distinct electrical patterns. AI algorithms learned to recognize these patterns, eventually allowing her to express sentences with over 95% accuracy.

"Open the window."

"I want some water."

"I want to see my family."

"I love you."

Though she couldn't move her lips, her inner voice reached the world once again.

However, this breakthrough hints at a deeper possibility: if specific brain signals can correspond to specific words, might specific external signals someday induce specific thoughts or emotions? Technology that reads the brain could one day talk back—and influence what we think.

Brain Mouse: Controlling a Cursor with Thought

Brain Mouse technology, designed for people with severe physical disabilities, enables users to move a computer cursor simply by thinking.

Israeli neurotech company MindMotion developed an affordable EEG-based headset that reads users' brain patterns and translates them into cursor movements and clicks.

When a user thinks "move left," the headset detects specific frequency patterns and converts them into coordinate signals.

Today, users can open files, browse the internet, write emails, and even play games—all without touching a mouse. Thought itself becomes the tool of action.

For users with paralysis, this technology is more than a device—it's a new set of "hands," allowing them to interact with the digital world using pure will.

MindMotion describes it best: "An interface that connects the freedom of thought with the real world."

Input BCI: Technology That Talks to the Brain

Technology is moving closer, growing quieter. Input BCIs allow machines to send signals into the brain. These signals can't be seen or touched, but they influence us—calming anxiety, sharpening focus, guiding emotions, or shifting decisions.

Machine → Brain.

The flow has begun.

tDCS: Disrupting Depression with Electricity

One man, battling moderate to severe depression, tried everything—therapy, medication—to no avail. Then he discovered tDCS: Transcranial Direct Current Stimulation. With tDCS, weak electrical currents (1-2mA) are applied to the scalp to stimulate specific brain regions. It's painless and subtle, but its impact can be profound.

He enrolled in a clinical trial, applying tDCS at home for 20 minutes a day, five days a week. At first, there was no noticeable change. But after a month, he found it easier to get out of bed. By the sixth week, emotional resilience returned. After ten weeks, he said:

"It wasn't a huge shift, but the weight got lighter, little by little. I felt like I could live again."

Similar studies, including large trials published in *Nature Medicine*, confirmed significant improvements in depression symptoms through tDCS.

tDCS represents a powerful, non-invasive BCI—gently reshaping neural circuits without entering the skull.

TMS: Magnetic Stimulation for PTSD Recovery

In a U.S. hospital, a veteran suffering from PTSD found traditional treatments ineffective. Then came TMS: Transcranial Magnetic Stimulation.

TMS uses magnetic fields, not implants, to target specific brain areas involved in emotion regulation. Researchers at Harvard showed that TMS could reduce the intensity of traumatic memories and rebuild emotional stability.

By delivering precisely timed magnetic pulses, TMS can regulate fear responses, demonstrating that even without surgery, external fields can reshape brain function.

DBS: Deep Brain Stimulation for Parkinson's Disease

In 2002, a man with Parkinson's underwent DBS surgery, implanting electrodes deep in his brain to regulate motor function.

The surgery was a success—he regained control over his movements. But he also experienced unexpected emotional swings: sudden anxiety, unexplained euphoria, and deep sadness.

Doctors confirmed that stimulating certain brain areas could influence not only movement but also mood, motivation, and emotional balance. DBS blurred the lines between treating symptoms and altering identity.

Non-Invasive Input BCI: Influence Without Implants

Many imagine mind control as something from science fiction, involving brain implants. But the greater threat is subtler: non-invasive input BCIs.

Without inserting anything, electromagnetic waves, low-frequency signals, and RF transmissions can still influence brain rhythms.

One woman reported headaches, insomnia, and surging anxiety at home—symptoms that mysteriously faded when she removed a smart speaker from her bedroom.

Today, it's possible to subtly alter brainwaves and emotional states using external signals—without the target's awareness.

Specific frequencies can induce anxiety, suspicion, impulsiveness, or emotional fatigue. And because these feelings arise internally, victims mistake them for their own emotions.

This invisible manipulation raises urgent ethical questions.

Emotions are pure—but they can be silently designed.

The Ethical Line Begins with Input BCI

Output BCI reads thoughts. The user remains the agent, and machines simply react.

Input BCI changes everything. Machines whisper to the brain—calming, agitating, shaping memories, nudging decisions.

Military experiments have suppressed fear responses. Marketing firms have tested emotionally priming consumers before ad exposure. Some labs are even experimenting with enhancing or erasing memories via targeted stimulation.

As the distance between brain and machine shrinks, the time we have to feel, hesitate, and freely choose may be shrinking too.

We must now ask: "Are these feelings truly mine?" Technology is moving closer, speaking more quietly, slipping deeper into the mind. It is no longer just about the "freedom to express thoughts"; it is about the "freedom to protect them."

This is the frontier we now face.

Part 2.

Living in an

Emotion-Tracking Society

Chapter 4. The Datafication of Emotion

Why Emotions Became the Target

If BCI technology connects the brain and machines, it's only natural that emotions are the first target. Emotions are our most immediate response to the world—they emerge before thoughts, before words. When we encounter a situation, we feel before we think. Fear, surprise, joy, and anger—these reactions fire off electrically in the amygdala and thalamus within milliseconds.

Technology targets emotions precisely because they arise fastest, are easiest to detect, and are most readily manipulated. When we feel anger, anxiety, joy, or sadness, our brainwave patterns shift. Heart rate, skin conductivity, and breathing rhythm—all change subtly.

Machines are now sophisticated enough to catch these micro-changes. While they can't yet fully decode complex thoughts or language, they can already read "an emotion has occurred" with impressive accuracy. Thus, machines began by reading emotions—and then, inevitably, by influencing them.

Emotions Aren't Just Feelings

Emotions aren't just feelings. They are the foundation of judgment. Humans don't make decisions without emotions. We don't think without first feeling. Emotions set the direction; thought builds the path.

If emotions can be manipulated, judgment changes, choices shift, and actions follow a different course. We often say:

"I don't know why I did that."

"I wasn't myself."

Sometimes it's not just overwhelming feelings—it may be that emotions were quietly induced from the outside. When that happens, it's not merely an emotional issue. It's a violation of free will.

Emotions arise first in the brain. They are the easiest for machines to read. They are the easiest to manipulate. And they are the bedrock of human autonomy. Every ethical debate about BCI technology ultimately boils down to this: Who owns your emotions?

Emotions Are Becoming a Tool for Consumption

In 2017, Walmart filed a patent for a system that analyzed customers' facial expressions and movements via in-store cameras. If a customer appeared frustrated at checkout, an employee would be alerted to intervene. This wasn't just about service—it was about reading and steering emotional flows in real time.

Amazon, that same year, began developing algorithms to recommend products based on users' facial expressions. Smiling? Suggest bright clothing. Tired? Offer relaxation products. Irritated? Push stress-relief items. Their "Echo Look" device, marketed as a fashion assistant, quietly doubled as a tool for emotional data collection.

Facebook operated even more quietly. Long before you clicked "Like," Facebook tracked your eye movements, scrolling speed, and mouse positioning to predict your emotional state. Leaked internal reports revealed experiments on monitoring teen users' moods and targeting ads at moments of low self-esteem—when loneliness or sadness made users most vulnerable.

China took it further. In 2018, Hangzhou Xiaoshan Airport deployed AI facial recognition to flag anxious, nervous, or suspicious individuals for security screening. Emotions became a threat signal. Emotion-reading became a tool of social control.

Walmart. Amazon. Facebook. Chinese airports. They all tell the same story:

"Machines know how you feel—before you do."

Emotions have become a strategy to sell, a weapon to control, and a resource to harvest. Emotion is no longer an internal experience. Emotion has become a product.

How Cameras Know Your Emotions

When we imagine "reading brainwaves," we often picture someone wearing electrodes. But reality is quieter. Smartphone cameras, laptop webcams, and store CCTVs— these devices don't just capture images. They analyze micro-muscle movements: eyebrow angles, lip twitches, eyelid tremors. From these subtle shifts, they infer joy, sadness, irritation, or anxiety.

And it's not just cameras. Smartwatches track pulse changes. Mouse movements reveal hesitation. Screen scrolling patterns reflect agitation or calm. Without speaking, without moving deliberately, our bodies are constantly broadcasting emotional clues.

Machines read these signs. They redesign our experiences. Different ads appear. Different content is promoted. Different discounts are offered—all triggered by emotional footprints we didn't even realize we left.

The Ethics of Inducing Emotions

If reading emotions sounds unnerving, inducing emotions demands even greater caution.

It's tempting to think: "Wouldn't it be nice if a machine adjusted to my feelings?" Playing soothing music when you're tired, suggesting meditation videos when you're sad. Convenient. Thoughtful.

But what if the machine begins deciding how you should feel? What if it nudges you toward purchases by amplifying your anxiety? What if it shapes your worldview by reinforcing selective emotional states?

At that point, your emotions are no longer truly yours. You believe you are feeling freely—but you might just be feeling what you were made to feel.

Chapter 5. BCI: Born to Heal

BCIs for Medical Healing in the 1970s

Every technology begins with a fundamental question.

Brain-Computer Interface (BCI) is no different. The

question was: "Can we transmit the thoughts of those who

can no longer move their bodies but are still thinking?"

In the 1970s, the first scientific experiment to address this

question began at UCLA (University of California, Los

Angeles). Researchers attached electrodes to the scalp and

began measuring brainwaves (EEG) in real time. For the

first time, they successfully translated these faint electrical

signals from the brain into visible data on a computer

screen. The moment when thoughts were first translated

into machine language was quiet but left a profound mark on the history of human communication.

From the beginning, BCI was a technology for recovery. Bodies that could no longer move. Voices that could no longer speak. Bodies that were shut off from the world, yet still inhabited by a living brain. The belief in that brain became the starting point for BCI.

In the 1980s and 1990s, research involving ALS (Amyotrophic Lateral Sclerosis) patients became active. Even people who couldn't move at all were found to produce subtle brainwave changes when they focused on specific words. Scientists began developing systems to communicate "yes" or "no" through brainwaves alone.

By the early 2000s, medical BCI expanded further. Studies began on controlling wheelchairs with brainwaves, moving cursors with intention alone, not using hands or eyes. We entered an era where the mind could restore motion to a paralyzed body. BCI wasn't just evolving as a tool. It became a technology that opened the hearts of those who couldn't speak, allowing them to communicate again.

Evolution of Medical BCI Over the Years

- 1973: UCLA in the U.S. begins EEG-based computer control experiments.
- 1980s-1990s: Attempts to communicate through thoughts with ALS patients.
- Early 2000s: Research into practical assistive devices like controlling wheelchairs and moving cursors with intention.
- 2010s: Experiments expand to controlling artificial limbs and exoskeletons.
- 2020s: Real-time typing, gaming, and language generation through brain implant chips.

The Beginning of Restoring Movement with Implantable Electrodes

One of the most notable real-world applications of BCI technology is DBS (Deep Brain Stimulation) for Parkinson's disease. Parkinson's causes the motor circuits in the brain to deteriorate, leading to symptoms like hand tremors, muscle rigidity, slow movements, and instability while walking. While medication can initially control these symptoms, the effectiveness diminishes as the disease progresses.

This is where DBS comes in. DBS involves implanting electrodes deep into the brain and sending tiny electrical impulses to restore movement. The electrodes stimulate motor-related brain circuits, such as the thalamus, basal ganglia, and subthalamic nucleus, to revive motor functions.

This technology was commercialized in the 1990s and is now used by hundreds of thousands of patients worldwide, including in the U.S., Europe, and South Korea. The DBS device includes a battery-powered controller that is also implanted in the body, and patients can adjust the stimulation intensity and patterns as needed. In essence, the brain responds to external machine settings. DBS has allowed patients who had been confined to a wheelchair for years to walk again, and individuals who couldn't write due to tremors can now write again.

Moving Machines with the Mind

In 2004, a team from Brown University in the U.S. successfully conducted the first clinical experiment to directly link a human brain to a computer. This project, called BrainGate, symbolized the opening of the "path where thoughts turn into movements."

The first participant was a man who had been paralyzed from the neck down due to an accident. He could no longer move any part of his body except his eyes and facial expressions. The researchers precisely opened his skull and implanted a microelectrode array, consisting of around 100 tiny electrodes, into the motor cortex of his brain. This device was designed to detect the faint electrical signals generated by the brain's intention to move.

A few days later, something incredible happened. He couldn't move his fingers, but when he thought, "I need to move," the cursor on the computer screen began to move. His hand remained still, but his thought was moving the cursor.

This wasn't a simple response. The computer read the brainwaves and detected the patterns associated with his thoughts—"I want to move the cursor in this direction," or "I want to select this word." The signals became commands, with his thoughts directly controlling the machine. Later, he used his brainwaves to send emails, select music, move a robotic arm, and lift a cup. No hand movements, no words spoken—only the signals generated in his brain.

Speaking Through Brainwaves

When we ask someone, "Are you okay?" and they can't respond with a gaze or a nod, how can we read their feelings?

A neuroscience team in Germany created a method to communicate with patients who could neither speak, gesture, nor blink. Their target was ALS patients—whose bodies are paralyzed, leaving them unable even to blink. However, their brains were still active, thinking, feeling, and reacting.

The researchers applied a non-invasive BCI, using EEG systems that attached electrodes to the scalp. Although these patients couldn't move, their brain responses subtly changed when asked a question. When they wanted to say "yes," an alpha wave response appeared in the frontal lobe and sensory cortex. When they wanted to say "no," beta waves were suppressed.

The responses were faint, like tiny brain gestures, but the machine could read them. This enabled patients to choose "yes" or "no" by thought alone, linking this decision-making to a text selection interface. With this device, they could write 20-30 characters per day. Slowly, but accurately. Quietly, but firmly. One patient even spent two days just to write "I love you" to his family. This experiment proved one thing: his brain was alive, and his mind could still reach out to the world.

Treating Depression, Anxiety, and Impulsiveness

BCI technology was initially developed to restore movement to immobile bodies. But now, it has quietly moved into a far more delicate area: the mind.

The first experiments targeting emotional circuits began at top research institutions like UCLA, Johns Hopkins, and Mount Sinai Hospital. They've started clinical trials using BCI to directly influence the emotional circuits of patients suffering from depression, PTSD, and impulse control disorders.

The process is surprisingly simple. It involves sending very mild electrical impulses to areas of the brain responsible for emotional regulation, such as the prefrontal cortex, amygdala (which handles fear responses), and the nucleus accumbens (linked to impulse control). These impulses are not intense electric shocks, but rather weak signals, almost imperceptible to the patient. Yet they're strong enough to alter the synaptic connections between neurons. It's like pressing a small button to slightly adjust the emotional balance.

The results were astonishing. People who were deeply depressed reported feeling lighter with each passing day. Those plagued by anxiety experienced unexpected calm. Impulsive behaviors dramatically decreased. Of course, this is still in the early stages. Not all patients show the same effects. But the key takeaway is clear: the technology to regulate emotions is no longer science fiction—it's medical reality.

For a long time, we believed that depression was a personal issue, anxiety a matter of personality, and impulsivity something we had to control ourselves. But these experiments are telling us a different story. A lot of what we call the "mind" is actually electrical currents flowing through our brain circuits. And these currents can be carefully adjusted and finely tuned.

Emotions are no longer off-limits. BCI technology is now not just about moving limbs, remembering things, or even restoring speech. It's starting to directly influence the flow of emotions. This is undoubtedly hopeful. For those suffering from depression and trauma, it could be a new treatment. But it also raises a question: "Is the emotion I'm feeling really mine? Or is someone quietly controlling it?"

Chapter 6. Why Did the Military Want to Control Emotions?

Emotions as Weapons of War

Brain-Computer Interface (BCI) technology began with a noble purpose: to help people. It allowed paralyzed patients to communicate through thoughts, enabling those who couldn't speak to express themselves again. The initial aim of BCI was to restore lost human functions.

However, the entities most interested in this technology were not medical institutions. Much faster than hospitals, there was another group that recognized BCI's potential: the military. It wasn't weapons manufacturers or drone design labs, but military psychological research institutes and defense technology agencies that saw BCI as a tool to design and control human emotions, judgment, and impulses.

The most unpredictable variable in warfare has always been the human element. Even trained soldiers experience fear before battle, make impulsive decisions, and sometimes hesitate or even sympathize with the enemy. More terrifying than a gun is the human mind's emotions.

The military's interest in BCI was simple: "Let's create a brain that moves exactly as ordered." A brain that could fire without fear, carry out orders without guilt, and aim without hesitation.

BCI was perfectly suited for this purpose. In fact, the military had been conducting research on "emotion-control BCIs," "focus-enhancement BCIs," and "neural-based training systems" under various names for decades. BCI was no longer just a technology that reads brain signals; it was evolving into a battlefield that designs the flow of emotions and judgments. And this silent battlefield was always starting inside the human mind.

U.S.: From Emotional Control to Tactical Judgment

In the early 2000s, DARPA (Defense Advanced Research Projects Agency) initiated a project called Neural-Based Battlefield System. The surface-level justification was simple: improve soldier protection and combat performance. But quickly, the focus evolved to controlling emotions and adjusting judgment.

Their concern was straightforward: When soldiers pull the trigger, give commands, or make split-second decisions, emotions like fear, anxiety, confusion, and impulse often cloud their judgment, leading to mistakes. The solution? "Can we block those emotions beforehand?"

Using EEG brainwave sensors, researchers tracked emotional responses in the amygdala and prefrontal cortex in real time. When a specific pattern was detected—for example, anxiety signals triggered by detecting a threat—the machine would send a feedback signal to suppress or reduce the emotional reaction. The results were remarkable. Soldiers reacted much more calmly and quickly in the same situations. Fear was diminished, and command execution improved. The dangerous fantasy of "emotionless soldiers" was quietly becoming a reality.

DARPA didn't stop there. Their next goal was even more radical: "Let's have the brain command the battlefield, not the hand holding the gun." They began experimenting with using brainwaves to control drones and simulate troop movements. Like a first-person shooter game, soldiers would control combat systems using only their brains, without needing their hands. DARPA named this project Cyborg Commander, a military soldier who commands in real-time with brainwave-generated decisions, targeting, and orders.

China: A Military That Reads Soldiers' Emotions

In 2018, the Chinese government issued special equipment to some military units, security personnel at power plants, and nuclear facilities. These helmets weren't just protective gear; they contained EEG sensors that monitored brainwaves in real time to analyze attention, fatigue, stress, fear responses, and aggression. The emotional data was transmitted directly to a central server, allowing managers to monitor the focus and mental state of soldiers or security personnel.

On the surface, the system appeared to be a "safety prevention system," designed to detect and prevent accidents by assessing fatigue or mental instability in critical security workers. But in practice, this technology began to be used as a tool to monitor emotions and control compliance. The system worked simply but chillingly: the emotional changes of the wearer were recorded as data and compared to a defined "acceptable emotional range." Any deviation—fatigue, tension, doubt, or even sadness—was flagged as an "abnormal response." Emotions were no longer free-flowing; they became subjects of control.

This experiment illustrated how human emotional flows can be transformed into something "monitored." Emotions, once free and unpredictable, could now be governed. This raises unsettling questions: "If we can read emotions, could we eventually regulate them?" "What happens when fear, anger, or doubt become forbidden, or when 'acceptable emotions' are defined by a system?"

We must not forget. This technology may begin as a "device to detect anxiety," but it could someday evolve into a "device to prevent anxiety." BCI is a technology that reads emotions. But depending on who uses it and for what purpose, emotions could easily become something controlled and prohibited.

Israel: Designing a Trauma-Free Battlefield

Israel has long been a country that prioritizes the "mind" over the "body" in its defense technologies. Decades of real-world military service and the ongoing PTSD cases among soldiers led the Israeli Defense Forces (IDF) to ask: "Can we fight without the mind getting injured?"

BCI technology quietly began answering this question. The IDF, in collaboration with private neuroscience startups, began experiments to help soldiers return from combat without emotional trauma. Their solution? Emotion Feedback Suppression Devices. These devices analyze EEG data from soldiers in real-time during training, and if anxiety, fear, or guilt signals appear, the device sends tiny electrical pulses to suppress these emotions before they can overwhelm the soldier.

The results were astounding. Soldiers with unwavering focus, steady eye contact, and no visible reaction during even the most brutal simulations. "They were more like mission-oriented systems than soldiers," noted an observer.

The goal of the system was to prevent trauma, but it ended up effectively shutting down the soldier's "emotional response circuits." A battlefield without emotion might be more efficient, but the ethical concerns surrounding such efficiency began to deepen.

Russia: Using Emotions to Dismantle the Enemy

Russia wasn't interested in simply suppressing or modulating emotions. Their focus was on a more strategic goal: "The most effective way to incapacitate the enemy is to make them incapable of making decisions."

Since the mid-2010s, Russia has developed a concept called Cognitive Paralysis Tactics as part of its military cyberwarfare strategy. The method was surprisingly simple: by analyzing the brainwave patterns of the enemy, Russia could identify collective decision-making rhythms formed in high-pressure situations or on the battlefield. They then used specific emotional stimuli, like audio, visual, or brainwave interference, to disrupt those rhythms. Within minutes, the enemy would become disoriented, miss commands, and make conflicting decisions. The result? Their command structure collapsed from within. Russia referred to this tactic as a "weapon that shakes the brain before the battle even starts."

This is no longer science fiction. BCI technology has silently expanded beyond just moving limbs or restoring speech. It now targets thought itself—manipulating decisions, controlling judgment, and altering the very way we think.

South Korea: Guarding Minds with Brainwaves

BCI technology is no longer just a distant concept from foreign countries. In South Korea, this technology is quietly but steadily advancing, particularly in defense and surveillance sectors.

One of the most prominent examples is the brainwave-based boundary response detection system. This system measures soldiers' brainwaves in real-time to automatically detect states of drowsiness, distraction, or excessive stress, and sends warnings accordingly. On the surface, this seems like a convincing and practical technology. If we can monitor someone's attention in real-time, it could help reduce accidents and increase responsiveness. But when you look deeper at the environments where this technology is applied, it's easy to see that its purpose may extend beyond just "monitoring attention."

In real-world scenarios, such as the military training at Kwangwoon University's Defense Industry Research Institute, brainwave monitoring is used to improve accuracy during shooting drills by tracking theta waves (drowsiness), beta waves (concentration), and alpha waves (relaxation). The potential of BCI-based target recognition technology was also showcased at a competition held by South Korea's Defense Acquisition Program Administration in 2024. This competition demonstrated the possibilities of reading human intentions or judgments through brainwaves, linking them to unmanned drones and surveillance systems.

BCI technology now holds the potential to control individuals without the need for physical weapons. Its development presents not just a leap forward in national defense but also a significant ethical challenge in defining the boundary between state and individual.

Chapter 7. The Powers That Design Emotions: Politics, Information, Religion, Society

Power Knows How to Steal Emotions

When we think of "control," we often imagine someone physically restraining our actions, silencing our voices, or dominating our movements. But today, control doesn't manifest so openly. Now, control operates quietly, within our emotions, our thoughts, and our very minds. People still believe they make their own judgments and choices. But what if the emotions they feel were designed first? Is that judgment really theirs?

This chapter aims to answer that question. We'll explore how political powers, intelligence agencies, tech companies, religions, and society—groups that appear completely different on the surface—have all transformed emotions into data and used it to manipulate reactions.

Political Power: Emotions Are Manipulated Before Votes

In 2019, during an election campaign in Central Europe, political strategists introduced a subtle but new tool. It wasn't a speech-writing program or a polling software. It was a BCI-based brainwave analyzer, eye-tracking devices, and emotion-response algorithms. The campaign's goal was clear: "Find the words that provoke the strongest emotional reaction with the fewest words."

The campaign recruited 120 participants, who wore small EEG devices while watching videos of the candidate's speeches or reading policy statements. The research team measured real-time changes in beta waves (concentration), gamma waves (excitement), and theta waves (anxiety) in the participants' brainwaves each time specific words or phrases appeared. They also tracked which words held the participants' gaze the longest.

The results were clear. Word combinations like "safety," "children," and "uncertainty" triggered anxiety and focus for most participants. On the other hand, words like "equality," "solidarity," and "cooperation" tended to relax them and reduce focus. Based on this data, the campaign revamped its messaging, shifting from themes of cooperation and hope to ones that stirred anxiety and personal crisis.

The final speech read: "We are living in times of crisis. Crime threatens our neighbors, and children's futures are no longer safe. If we do not choose today, someone else will decide for us tomorrow."

On the surface, this message appealed to a sense of crisis, but in reality, the sentences were carefully crafted based on neurological data to provoke maximum emotional responses. The candidate wasn't just delivering a message; they were pressing the emotional buttons inside the audience's minds.

Voters' reactions were telling: "This candidate is speaking exactly what I've been feeling." "They're saying what I've been worried about." "I can't support anyone else this time." However, these feelings didn't arise naturally; they were the result of carefully engineered neural responses. BCI technology didn't just collect data; it designed the flow of emotions and, through those emotions, influenced behavior.

In 2022, during an election in another Eastern European country, a progressive candidate, who had strong support for education and welfare policies, was doing well in interviews, public hearings, and local events. However, at some point, the candidate's social media algorithms began to subtly change.

Edited videos of the candidate's past statements began circulating. They showcased moments of wavering speech, hesitant gestures, and awkward pauses. These videos were repeatedly shown. The content was emotionally designed—based on emotional response data—to focus on moments of discomfort, anger-inducing phrases, and scenes that triggered emotional reactions.

The campaign's objective wasn't to criticize the candidate directly, but to achieve something much more refined: "Make people feel a slight sense of rejection when they think of this person." "Make their brain react with tension when they hear their name."

When emotions shift, all information begins to appear differently. "The policies sound fine, but something feels off." "What they said seems right, but I don't trust them." "Can I really trust this person with the country?"

These aren't logical doubts; they are emotional responses. This aligns perfectly with what BCI research describes: "Emotion precedes judgment, and emotional responses precede later reactions."

Long-time supporters even expressed, "That person isn't bad, but... I just feel uneasy now. I don't really know why." This was proof that emotional manipulation had worked. The information hadn't changed, but the brain's response to it had.

BCI is not just a piece of technology. It is a philosophy based on emotion datafication, emotional prediction, and emotional manipulation. This case shows how such a philosophy can be applied in politics. On the surface, it appears to be a free choice, but the emotions behind that choice had already been quietly designed.

Information Power: The Spy Hidden in Your Emotions

It's not even necessary to touch the brain to influence emotions. For years, intelligence agencies have been monitoring people. But since the mid-2010s, surveillance has expanded beyond mere observation. Now, surveillance involves tracking and intervening in the feelings, shifts, and breakdowns occurring inside the person in real time.

In 2010, NSO Group, an Israeli security tech company, developed Pegasus, spyware that perfected this silent intervention. Pegasus can infiltrate a smartphone without even a single click. It accesses the camera, microphone, location data, call logs, and message history—everything in real-time. Even when the phone appears to be off, the spyware quietly observes the emotional responses of the target.

The scariest part of this technology is its focus not on what the person said, but on the moments when they didn't speak. Silence, hesitation, emotional unease—this is where the emotional amplitude is read.

A human rights activist in the Middle East expressed emotional fatigue and anxiety in private messages before publishing an article criticizing the government. Pegasus collected that data. A few days later, photos of his daughter and personal messages were shared by an anonymous account. He didn't make official complaints or write articles. He simply stepped back. While no one could say exactly what happened, his psychological state had been read, and the timing of his public attack had been strategically set.

In 2021, a female member of the Spanish Parliament discovered that her smartphone had been infected by Pegasus. Leading up to the election campaign, she experienced extreme sleep deprivation, emotional instability, and increased aggression. Repeated mistakes during the campaign led to a sharp drop in her support. Upon investigation, it was revealed that her sleep patterns, heart rate rhythms, and message interruptions had all been silently collected. These "message interruptions"—when she paused or stopped typing during conversations— became a key indicator of emotional shifts or psychological states. Spyware or emotional analysis systems record these gaps in time and precisely analyze when someone's mind faltered. At the most unstable moments, threatening messages from the opposition, media scandals, and psychological pressure were perfectly timed and spread. Eventually, she ended her campaign. Not due to fatigue or anxiety, but because she couldn't withstand the psychological strain. Only later did she discover that all her emotional reactions had been digitally intervened with.

We often think of BCI as technology that requires electrodes in the brain. But these examples show us that emotional states can be read and manipulated through digital signals alone, without touching the brain itself. With this data, emotions can be quietly induced, leading to behavior changes without the need for direct physical manipulation.

Pegasus didn't touch the body, but the emotional shifts in the target's mind were undoubtedly recorded in the data flow. No one called it "emotional invasion." No one reported "hacked emotions." The conversation was hacked, but anxiety couldn't be reported, and vigilance became no more than evidence. Emotions existed outside the law, and technology quietly breached that boundary.

Pegasus didn't just steal information. It read emotional states, planned the optimal moments for intervention, and analyzed the responses post-intervention. This perfectly mirrors the BCI goal of "emotion feedback → behavior influence." The difference? No physical machine device was involved. Pegasus was a digital neural intervention system without BCI equipment. And it was the quietest and most effective form of emotional control.

Religious Power: Engineering Awe

Religion deals with some of the deepest human emotions: guilt, awe, and a sense of salvation. These emotions are so powerful that it's hard to explain them in words. As a result, people believe they are "genuine." But here, we ask the question: "Was that emotion truly something that arose naturally from within me, or was it something someone made me feel?"

In 2018, a new religious group in East Asia quickly attracted followers by offering a "spiritual healing experience." The official explanation was simple: "Repentance occurs through the power of words." However, testimonies from ex-members and academic investigations revealed a complex emotional manipulation system hidden behind the scenes.

- Slow-tempo piano and voice prompts for breathing were played simultaneously.
- Words like "sin," "forgiveness," and "let go" were repeated, and screen transitions occurred with each phrase.

These devices monitored the emotional responses of the followers—tears, heart rate, silence followed by crying—and adjusted accordingly.

"In that moment, I collapsed. I didn't even know what sin I had committed, but I just cried." — Testimony from an ex-member

He cried, knelt, and stood up, saying, "Now I am a new person." But that emotion was, in fact, part of a system-designed flow.

One large religious organization created a VR experience of sacred texts. Followers virtually "met God" while listening to a large choir, seeing 3D images of ancient holy sites, and hearing deep, grand pipe organ music. At that moment, brainwave sensors recorded their emotional responses.

Time spent bowing, tear secretion, pupil dilation, and gamma waves (engagement) were all collected in real-time.

The scenes with the highest engagement were inserted again at the next worship service.

"It wasn't an experience of meeting God. It was just a technology that made me believe I had met God." — Confession of a VR designer involved in the project

Some cults repeatedly fed their followers these messages: "Your sins have harmed the community." Then, in front of all the followers, they made them kneel and "confess their sins." Dramatic transitions followed:

- The leader approaches, lays hands on them, and declares, "You are forgiven."
- All lights turn on, and the sounds of praise burst forth as people weep and cheer.

This process completes the emotional curve of "fear → shame → salvation → gratitude → loyalty."

The follower says, "I am saved." But that emotion was likely the result of meticulously designed emotional stimuli.

- Emotional response collection: Tears, breathing, sweating, response time tracking
- Emotional pattern analysis: Identifying which sermon tones trigger strong reactions

- Emotional stimulus design: Using trigger words and sound structures learned through repetition
- Behavior induction: Encouraging repentance, donations, obedience, and isolated loyalty

When this design is successful, the person believes that emotion is "theirs." This is the most silent and most dangerous emotional infringement. If what I believed to be genuine emotion was actually created by someone else—who am I, and what are my beliefs?

Social Power: Our Emotions May Not Have Been Ours

In 2020, a national "mental health recovery campaign" was launched in one country. The slogan was warm: "Everyone is tired. Let's empathize together." Posters were displayed on the streets, and famous actors sent messages of encouragement via social media. People expressed gratitude for the emotional comfort they received. On the surface, the campaign seemed to embrace everyone with positive energy.

But one day, a private research institute raised a cautious question: "Is this campaign really meant for everyone's comfort?" Upon analyzing the campaign structure, the research found it to be far more intricate than anticipated. First, people encountered hashtags reminding them of the feeling of being "tired" dozens of times a day: #Just_Holding_On_Today, #It's_Okay_To_Be_Tired_Too, #You're_Not_The_Only_One_Struggling. These phrases naturally filled the feeds. At first, they felt comforting, but over time, people began to internalize the idea that "being tired" was normal and "enduring" became a given emotional state.

Video content reinforced this emotional trend. Slow-paced narration, soft piano music, and the message "It's okay not to speak" were played. Between news, ads, subway TVs, and mobile app clips, people passed by these videos without much thought, but the background music and rhythm of language slowly seeped into their minds. Moreover, the campaign included interactive surveys asking people to record "their emotions." "How did you feel today?" "Describe the moment you felt most exhausted." At the end of each day, people wrote down feelings like "overwhelmed," "helpless," and "I don't want to speak." Unknowingly, they kept reminding themselves of "the tired me."

The result was subtle but clear. Complaints on the streets decreased, participation in social issues dropped, and people began to accept "nothing will change even if I speak up." It wasn't about suppressing anger or erasing frustration. It was simply about aligning everyone into a singular "tired state."

Around the same time, a similar trend was observed in an educational community. The phrase "Watching is also an act of harm" seemed to be righteous. But behind it lay a structure that forced emotional obligation: "If you remain silent, someone might be hurt," "If you don't share this message, you are an onlooker."

People instantly felt guilty. Hesitation became irresponsibility, neutrality became cowardice, and even the desire to rest quietly was branded as "inhuman."

These phrases weren't just campaign tools. The text structure, color schemes, and repeating patterns were all emotional stimuli strategies based on emotional reaction experiments. People believed they were thinking for themselves, but the emotional flow had already quietly been designed to follow a predetermined path.

Why Was It Quiet? The Silent Contract of Technology and Power

Every emotional manipulation system worked quietly. And all those in power kept that silence intact. Technology measured people's emotions, sometimes induced them, and in some cases, completely imposed emotions onto them. But at that moment, no one—the observer, the system recording the data, the expert detecting the patterns—spoke out.

There were reports of emotional collapse among participants in public experiments. Yet, the ethics committee concluded, "No physical harm occurred, and voluntary consent was obtained, so there is no ethical issue." They dismissed the existence of the report, citing that "emotional trauma" was not documented.

Journalists knew. They knew about the Pegasus infiltration scenario, campaign framing, and emotion-triggering interfaces... but they couldn't write the headlines. "There's no proof." "People won't believe it." "Critical articles on technology don't get views." Even as people's emotions were manipulated, the media refrained from reporting it, citing "lack of proof."

Some researchers knew as well. They realized their brainwave experiments weren't just simple cognitive response tests, but preliminary data for collective emotional manipulation experiments. But they quietly wrote papers, quietly submitted grant requests, and quietly recruited more participants. "We're just researching the future of technology." "Interpreting emotions is up to the interpreter."

Technology wasn't transparent. Power took advantage of that opacity. This is what we call the silent contract. Technology claimed it could measure emotions, but it never spoke about how it could destroy a person. Power used that technology without asking how it left emotional traces. And we continued to live, without ever discerning whether the emotions that stirred us were truly ours or whether they had been designed by technology.

Ethics committees, the media, academia—they were silent. "In the name of technology, inhuman things happened, but no one spoke." Technology was opaque, and power took advantage of that opacity.

Chapter 8. How the Human Brain Became a Commodity

Your Emotions Are the Prey of Advertising

Advertising used to have a simple goal: "Catch the eye." Ads evolved to be bigger, brighter, faster, and more stimulating. But now, advertising no longer simply aims to show—it seeks to read your emotions and unconscious mind.

In 2023, a neuro-marketing startup, Neuro-Insight, collaborated on an ad campaign for a global sports brand. Participants wore small EEG headsets while watching TV ads. The device measured real-time brainwave responses, eye movements, stress levels, and heart rate changes.

During one scene, when a young man ran toward a cliff and jumped, participants' brainwaves spiked with patterns of "anticipation" and "engagement." But when the product logo appeared immediately after, the emotional response dropped significantly. The ad team then adjusted the timing of the logo's appearance to coincide with the peak emotional response.

Now, emotion-based feedback is not just about analyzing viewership; it's about reading and adjusting unconscious reactions.

Emotion-based ad analysis works like this:

1. Measuring viewer brainwaves and biometric signals (EEG, eye-tracking, skin conductivity, heart rate analysis)

2. Analyzing emotional responses to each scene (engagement, interest, stress reactions, signs of disengagement)

3. Real-time ad scenario modification (shorten tension points, lengthen positive points—insert the brand at emotional peaks)

4. Creating customized versions (automatically generating different ads based on age, gender, emotional tendencies)

This technology is no longer just about creating efficient ads. It shows how precisely consumer emotions and unconscious minds can be manipulated. We no longer live in an era where we watch ads. We live in an era where ads read us, react to us, and manipulate us.

In 2022, Facebook began offering Emotion AI-based real-time ad adjustments to some advertisers. It analyzed subtle facial muscle movements through the front camera to assess emotional reactions and automatically optimized the timing and content of ads. Advertisers could now show discount codes when a user smiles, or expose the next product when they look surprised. Even your smile became a target for marketing.

Now, ads are reading your brainwaves, your eye movements, and your emotional state. This technology is wrapped under the label of personalization, but in reality, it signals an era where corporations own your unconscious mind. Emotion-based feedback systems have moved beyond efficient marketing and can intrude on an individual's empathy rights and privacy. We now face the question: "Are your emotions still yours?"

Neuromarketing: Tracking Brainwaves, Eyes, and Emotions

A global streaming platform quietly began a new experiment. Ostensibly, it was about "recommending more engaging content," but in reality, emotional curve analysis was being conducted based on user viewing data. The platform didn't attach sensors to users' brains like BCI systems. But what they were doing was eerily similar to BCI technology.

The system doesn't read users' emotions directly. It doesn't say, "You're happy" or "You're sad." But it reads unconscious behaviors: when users stop playback, the timing of swipes, and how they move their heads while watching. These unconscious actions are interpreted as signals of emotional reactions.

The data is interpreted as follows:

- "Many users tilted their heads during this scene" → boredom

- "There was almost no eye movement during this scene"
  → engagement or tension
- "Video exit rates significantly increase after midnight"
  → fatigue or loss of focus

From users' behavioral data alone, emotional flows can be precisely predicted. Based on these predictions, the platform calculates "what stimulus will be most effective for this person right now" and automatically adjusts content recommendations or edits. Users feel like they simply watched something they wanted, but in reality, they are walking along an emotional flow designed by algorithms. This system doesn't directly read emotions—it estimates and induces emotional flows, working structurally just like BCI.

Netflix's opening experiment clearly demonstrated this process. In 2021, Netflix created three versions of an opening sequence for a drama:

1. Suspenseful music + close-ups of characters
2. Quick cut transitions + strong visual stimuli
3. Slow narration-centered opening

Participants wore small EEG headsets and eye-tracking devices while watching each version.

Results:

- Version 1: Highest emotional engagement (EEG data)
- Version 2: Highest eye focus (eye-tracking data)
- Version 3: Highest retention rate (behavioral data)

Based on this data, Netflix adjusted the opening sequences for different countries:

- U.S. users: Version 1 (high suspense)
- South Korean users: Version 3 (slow narration)

Content is now re-edited based on your emotional response data. Combining BCI, eye-tracking, and emotional response data, neuro-marketing has evolved into a technology that designs emotional flows rather than just ads or recommendations.

The question is no longer simple: "Are our emotions a right to be protected, or are they just data?" "Why did I like this product?" "Was clicking really my choice?" If emotional data is hidden behind our choices, whose emotions are they? Mine? Or the company's? This is the most profound dilemma of the neuro-marketing age.

TikTok, Netflix, YouTube: Algorithms That Move You

Every day, we open YouTube. We believe we're choosing "what we want to watch," clicking one of the recommended videos. But was that choice truly ours? In reality, our scroll speed, click timing, how long we stay on a video, and even that brief hesitation are all converted into emotional cues. And the algorithm quietly reads those emotional traces. TikTok works like this. It tracks how long users watch a video, when they swipe, and how long they linger without reacting. These tiny reaction patterns are combined to model the user's emotional curve. For example, at the end of a tiring day, users spend more time on slow-motion background music videos with emotional subtitles, while they quickly react to energetic dance videos or ASMR content when stressed. TikTok uses this data to infer "what emotional state is this person in" and recommends the videos that best match those emotions.

Netflix is even more sophisticated. If a user clicks on a drama and exits within 10 seconds, Netflix doesn't just mark it as "uninteresting."

- Thumbnail click time: If hesitation is long, it analyzes as "internal conflict."

- Exit time: A 10-second exit is interpreted as "expectation vs. reality discrepancy."
- Content watched after exiting: It reads this as an effort to "correct emotional imbalance."

Netflix combines these three indicators to determine what emotional expectations were present when a user clicked on the content and how those expectations shifted once the content started. As a result, Netflix no longer just recommends based on taste—it now designs content flows based on emotional scenarios.

YouTube has evolved too. In the past, only "watch time" mattered, but now it focuses on more detailed data:

- Time to click → Hesitation length = intersection of expectation and fear
- Time spent on the freeze-frame → Concentration or emotional trigger traces
- Comments + typing speed → Emotional engagement or impulsiveness indicators

This precise data doesn't just decide "which videos should be shown more"; it's used to predict "who you are" and "what emotional state you're in." The freedom of choice is shrinking, and emotions are being consumed.

The essence of content recommendation has shifted:

- In the past: "If you liked this content, you might also like this."
- Now: "Given your current emotional state, this will suit you best."

Content platforms now read your mood first. And they work to keep you in that emotional state for as long as possible by showing you content that reacts to your emotions.

Private Companies Upgrading the Brain

We often think of BCI technology as only for treating brain diseases like dementia or for neural rehabilitation. But right now, around the world, BCI technologies aimed at enhancement rather than recovery are quietly being developed. These technologies target more than just the medical market—they aim to make normal brains smarter. The key word in this market is cognitive enhancement. Concentration, memory, reaction speed, decision-making ability, and stress resilience—these are qualities that were once left to individual differences. But with the development of BCI technology, there is now a belief that we can actually improve brain function, which has led to real products and investments.

Kernel – Extracting Brain Data

Kernel, a U.S.-based neurotechnology company, is a leading player in cognitive enhancement BCI. They say, "We raise the resolution of the brain." The meaning is simple: just as we get clearer images when photos have more pixels, the more densely, quickly, and accurately we read the brain's data, the more clearly we can track emotional states, judgments, focus, and conscious flows. Kernel's Kernel Flow is a non-invasive BCI helmet that measures brain blood flow, oxygen saturation, and electrical signals. It analyzes in real-time how sensitive a user is to different stimuli, when their focus peaks, and when their emotional responses dramatically change. Kernel plans to apply this technology in education, sports, business, military strategy simulations, and other decision-making environments. They aim to accumulate brain response data and use that data to "train and guide" the brain. This is not just a technology for reading the brain—it's the first step in designing the brain.

Emotiv – From Focus Games to Talent Recruitment

Emotiv, a U.S.-Australian joint venture, is another leading consumer BCI company, having sold hundreds of thousands of BCI devices. Their flagship product, Emotiv Insight, is a brainwave measurement headset. Users wear this device and connect it to a computer, where they can monitor real-time data on concentration, relaxation, stress responses, and emotional fluctuations.

Interestingly, this technology is used not only in education but also in gaming and even HR companies. Some global talent recruitment platforms have started using Emotiv's equipment to measure candidates' concentration, judgment responses, and stress endurance. Companies say, "We trust the brain's real tendencies, not the resume." Whether this promise is trustworthy or the beginning of surveillance remains unclear, but what is clear is that the "era of brain data-based judgment" has begun.

Now, the brain is no longer just a target for recovery. BCI technology is increasingly being redefined by more and more companies as a tool for enhancing brains, not for "moving from abnormal to normal," but for "moving from normal to optimal." But we must ask ourselves: "Does the belief that the brain can be enhanced turn into an intangible pressure for all of us to improve?" "Will a society that says my brainwaves are behind, rather than that I lack focus, emerge?"

The Age of Brainwave-Based Education

In a kids' café in Gangnam, Seoul, children quietly sit with small headbands on. There are no VR goggles, no keyboards. They are just focusing. Something amazing happens. The more one child concentrates, the character on the screen starts running forward. Without moving or touching anything, simply by focusing, the game is controlled.

This device analyzes alpha waves (relaxation) and beta waves (concentration) in real-time. If alpha waves dominate, the brain is in rest mode; if beta waves dominate, information processing and concentration are active. The child's brainwave patterns are used to calculate a concentration score, which automatically adjusts the game's character's speed, direction, and level.

To the child, it feels like simple play. But for the educator, it's becoming a new tool to quantify invisible abilities like attention span, emotional stability, and response control.

Small BCI-based educational devices are quietly becoming commercially available worldwide.

Neurosky (USA) has released a home-use EEG headset called MindWave. It connects to brain training games, math problem-solving apps, and concentration music apps. Parents can monitor their child's brainwave status in real time. For example, if beta waves spike while solving a math problem, it's interpreted as "increased concentration"; if alpha waves rise, it signals "fatigue." Parents are now adjusting their child's study progress based on brainwave graphs rather than facial expressions.

Focus1 (China) has launched EEG devices for school group classes. Teachers can monitor students' concentration levels in real-time through a classroom monitor. Warnings such as "Class 3's concentration is dropping rapidly" or "Need to switch subjects in 5 minutes" are displayed.

AeyeTracker (Korea) is a startup that combines eye-tracking and brainwave analysis. They are conducting research for early ADHD diagnosis and providing concentration coaching programs for kindergartens and elementary schools. They analyze how often a child's gaze deviates and which stimuli hold their attention the longest, providing individualized concentration training.

All these trends point in one direction: "The brain is no longer invisible." The brain is being read, measured, and managed. This quiet shift raises new questions: "Who defines what makes a child 'good at studying'?" "Who decides that a child with high concentration is 'excellent'?" "Is brainwave data really about understanding children, or is it about assessing and classifying them?" BCI technology reads the brain—and quietly starts rewriting the standards of children's potential and limitations.

Chapter 9. Technology Knows Your Emotions

We Are Wired to BCI Without Devices

When we think of BCI (Brain-Computer Interface) technology, we often imagine scenes from sci-fi movies where electrodes are attached to the brain to control something. However, without such advanced devices, we are already living in a BCI system. Modern BCIs no longer rely solely on machines that read brainwaves. Our emotions, focus levels, behavior patterns, hesitation, and even withdrawal responses—all of our digital traces—become signals, data, and are silently interpreted.

For example, when you start typing a comment on an unpleasant post on social media, the platform can read your "annoyance":

- Increased number of backspaces → emotional agitation
- Rapid typing speed → increased impulsivity
- Short sentences, strong words → predicts signs of anger

The platform records and learns from this data. And then, it displays content that evokes the same emotion again. What we might have expected was, "After seeing something unpleasant, a soothing post will appear," but the platform makes the opposite decision: "Let's trigger this emotion again."

We believe we clicked on the content ourselves. But now we must ask: "Did I choose this content?" "Or was my emotion already designed by the algorithm?"

We didn't wear a brainwave measurement device, but the speed of our scrolling, hesitation, click timing, and even blinking—all of these unconscious traces already describe our brain state. We haven't worn BCI, but the logic and structure of BCI have already enveloped us. And now, our emotions are laid out on the palm of technology.

Technology Has Been Recording Your Emotions

One morning, you woke up as usual. The sunlight coming through the window was slightly dim, and your mind felt strangely heavy. As you drank your coffee and looked at your watch, the smartwatch quietly vibrated. A small message appeared on the screen: "Your stress level is higher than usual. Take a deep breath."

At that moment, you felt a sense of confusion and mild fear. "Does this device know how I feel?" You didn't say anything, didn't vent your frustration, nor complain to anyone. You just sat there. Yet, the machine knew. It knew that your breathing was shallower and faster than usual, that your heartbeat was slightly irregular, that you had turned over multiple times during your sleep and hadn't slept deeply.

That small wrist device had quietly gathered all those signals, and now it was advising you on your mood. "You are tense right now. It's a good idea to rest for a while." And now, the question changes: "Am I using this device?" "Or is this device reading me?"

You live your day. You go to work, meet people, relax. But technology, without you noticing, is predicting your mood, adjusting your behavior, and sometimes, guiding your choices.

Now Emotions Are Calculated in Numbers

One ordinary morning, as you wore your smartwatch and headed to work, you looked at your face in the elevator mirror. You hadn't felt particularly tired, but something seemed off. At that moment, the watch quietly vibrated. "Stress level: 74 / 100. Higher than usual."

A brief follow-up message appeared: "Try deep breathing for 3 minutes."

That short notification was telling you something about your body and mind before you even realized it: you were already carrying weight, even if you hadn't noticed.

This small watch was essentially scanning your subtle physiological signals in real-time. Even the emotional state you hadn't consciously noticed, the device had already detected.

How is this possible?

1. Heart Rate Variability (HRV):
   o Measures the small gaps between heartbeats.

- The gap narrows under tension and spreads during relaxation.
- A decrease in HRV is a key indicator of stress.

2. Galvanic Skin Response (GSR):
   - Measures the sensitivity of the skin to electrical currents to capture sweat responses, stress, and surprise reactions.

3. Sleep Pattern Analysis:
   - Tracks not just the sleep duration but also REM sleep ratio, deep sleep duration, turning over frequency, and changes in breathing rhythm, predicting mental fatigue and depression risks.

4. Stress Score / Fatigue Index:
   - Combines all the collected data and visualizes the user's emotional state in numbers.

A CEO from a Silicon Valley startup wore the Oura Ring, a smart ring, for several months to manage his sleep and fatigue. After finishing a typical busy day, he went to bed. He felt "fine." But the Oura Ring disagreed.

The next day, the app notified him: "Last night your heart rate was faster than usual, and your breathing was shallow and irregular. Recovery score: 42. Recommended: Reduce focused work today and relax."

That day, he paused and reflected on his day. Team conflicts, a failed investment meeting, a small argument with his wife… He had believed he was "handling it well," but the device had already detected the emotional accumulation.

Wearable devices' emotion-tracking functions give us a new tool for self-awareness. By confirming the signals our bodies send, we can view our condition more objectively. But, at the same time, we may be silently heading toward a society where our emotions are evaluated like report cards.

Emotion Control Without Us Knowing

We often believe we can hide our emotions. We smile even when we're angry, nod when we're bored, and say "I'm fine" even when we're uncomfortable. But now, technology goes beyond that "outward appearance"—it reads subtle traces like our breathing, eye movements, typing rhythms, and mouse movements.

These small signals are captured by emotion analysis systems. An "Emotion Analysis API" translates the traces we unconsciously leave into emotional signals, which are then sent in real-time to companies. And those emotional signals quietly become the raw materials for designing your behavior.

AI in Call Centers—"Just Before You Get Annoyed"
A global insurance company integrated an emotion analysis system into its AI call center. By analyzing the pitch of voices, silences between words, and changes in tone at the end of sentences, the system predicted when customers were about to express frustration. A small hesitation, like "Ah… so…" would trigger the system. The agent is immediately switched, and the problem-solving script adjusts. Emotions weren't spoken, but they were detected and responded to.

Shopping Mall UX—"When You Hesitate, the Price Drops"
An electronics online store analyzes mouse movements and scrolling patterns to capture signals of "purchase hesitation." When a user lingers on a product page for more than 17 seconds, leaves items in their cart without checking out, or zooms in on images, a suggestion appears at the top of the screen: "Get 10% off if you purchase now (limited for 30 minutes)." You think you made the decision because

of the discount, but in reality, your hesitation triggered the discount offer. Your hesitation was silently read and utilized by the system.

Meetings Even Read Your Focus

A global SaaS company integrated an emotion analysis system into Zoom video calls. It analyzes participants' facial expressions, eye movements, head angles, and blink speed to quantify engagement and emotional reactions. Specific slides show a drop in focus, while others see a sharp rise in positive reactions. This data is used to adjust meeting scripts and plan strategies for the next meeting. You attended the meeting, but your emotions had already become part of the system.

Understanding and Protecting Your Emotions

After a long workday, your smartphone quietly notifies you: "Today's fatigue score: 82 / 100." Immediately, your feed is filled with soothing mood videos, healing snack ads, and emotional release apps. The device seems to tell you to "rest."

But in reality, it's using your fatigue to keep you engaged longer and direct you toward consumption. Your fatigue is not a signal to rest but the perfect timing for consumption. What seems like comfort is, in fact, strategy. When we feel technology is understanding us, we must be wary of that very trust.

- Who is reading this data?
- From whose perspective is it being interpreted?
- Is that interpretation for my benefit or someone else's?

Technology is never neutral. Even when we do nothing, technology reads our state, reacts, and directs us. But whether that direction is for my benefit or someone else's goals, we will never know unless we consciously recognize it.

Now we must ponder: What emotional state was I in when I consumed this content? Is this emotion truly mine? Is technology helping me, or making me consume? The moment we ask those questions, we cease being objects of data. We must live as subjects of our own emotions.

To Protect Your Emotions, Know Them First

Is this emotion I'm feeling truly mine, or was it induced? The emotion you're feeling right now—is it truly yours? Or was it a fleeting video on YouTube last night, or a phrase that appeared on Instagram moments ago, that slightly twisted your mood?

We are now living in an era where emotions are consumed, designed, and induced. In the past, emotions were purely "a matter of the heart." But today, emotions are used as behavioral data, as reactions that fuel platform algorithms. You don't have to like something, comment, or even watch a video until the end. The time you spent, the movement of your eyes, the hesitation in your fingers—all of these leave traces of your emotional state. And those emotions are quietly stored, shaping the next piece of content you'll see. We install security apps, change passwords, and work hard to protect our personal information. But how much do we protect our emotional information?

- Where did my emotions originate today?
- Did I create my mood, or was it designed for me?
- In what state am I most likely to click and consume?

These questions are no longer philosophical thoughts. They are practical defenses for digital survival. Technology is increasingly centered around emotions. The sense we need to cultivate is not heightened sensitivity, but clear awareness:

- The strength to reflect on the source of our emotions, whether we're happy or sad
- The power to recognize whether that excitement while watching an ad is truly our desire, or a crafted reaction
- The ability to identify where our feelings come from before clicking on a comment

This is the first step in becoming the owner of our emotions.

Every day, you face a small crossroads: "Is the emotion I'm feeling truly mine?" Only those who repeatedly ask this question can survive as subjects in the digital BCI era, not as objects.

Part 3.

The Neuroscience of Emotion

Chapter 10. When Electrical Signals Turn Into Emotions

Emotions Can Be Measured

For a long time, we believed emotions to be something inexplicable. They rush in unexpectedly, are uncontrollable, and sometimes burst out in ways we cannot even comprehend. Therefore, emotions have been considered the ultimate proof of our humanity, a symbol of autonomy. But neuroscience and brain engineering view emotions in an entirely different light.

Emotions are not just "feelings." They are measurable flows created by electrical signals in the brain, chemical reactions involving hormones and neurotransmitters, and specific circuits that activate in response to stimuli. In other words, emotions have become something that can be read through physical structures. And the question now changes: "If emotions can be measured, can they also be artificially created?" It is at this point that BCI technology moves beyond measuring emotions to opening the door to manipulating them.

How Brain Circuits Create Feelings

We often say we feel emotions in our "hearts" or "minds," but in reality, emotions are born in the brain—not in just one place, but in multiple circuits simultaneously. Emotions don't start from a single button. Rather, they are an intricate electrical response in which multiple switches are pressed at the same time. And this process happens astonishingly fast and accurately.

It's 11 p.m. in a familiar neighborhood alley, on your way home after work. Suddenly, you spot a strange shadow standing still. Nothing has happened yet. The shadow doesn't move. But your heart rate increases, you stop walking, and you grip the keys in your hand. Where does this response begin?

Amygdala — The Alarm of Emotions

The first to respond is the amygdala. Before visual information even reaches the cerebral cortex, it quickly detects signals that seem threatening and immediately triggers a warning: "That could be dangerous." "Don't move." "Prepare to flee."

This decision isn't a rational analysis. It's an emotional reflex for survival. The reason the body reacts before you even fully recognize the face is because emotions are faster, and this speed comes from the purpose of survival.

Prefrontal Cortex — Social Regulation of Emotions

Next to activate is the prefrontal cortex. After receiving the amygdala's reaction, the prefrontal cortex decides whether to suppress it: "Is this really dangerous?" "Am I overreacting?" "Maybe running will make it worse."

The prefrontal cortex interprets, adjusts, and controls emotions. It is why, even when we're scared, we can refrain from running and pretend "it's fine."

Hippocampus — The Circuit That Brings Up Emotional Memories

At the moment of seeing the shadow, the hippocampus starts retrieving past memories. The memory of being pickpocketed in the same alley a few months ago. The footsteps you heard that day, the fear you felt, and how you avoided walking in that alley for a while afterward.

The hippocampus says: "This is a similar situation. Be careful." "Don't let it turn out like before." Past emotions are layered onto the present moment, amplifying your current emotions.

The amygdala, prefrontal cortex, and hippocampus—these three circuits play different roles but work together in a split second.

- The emotion is triggered quickly (Amygdala)
- The emotion is analyzed (Prefrontal Cortex)
- It is linked to past memories and interpreted (Hippocampus)

As a result, we decide whether to flee, approach, speak, or remain silent. And this entire process often happens before we even say "I felt an emotion."

This is why emotions can be designed. The flow of circuits that generate emotions is already being experimentally traced and controlled by neuroscience and BCI technology. What areas activate when specific emotions are induced, what electrical signals or feedback can suppress those emotions, and how the connection between memory and emotion can reconstruct trauma—technology has started explaining all of this. Emotions are no longer just "pure." They are becoming structures that can be read, calculated, and even manipulated.

Electrical Signals Create Emotional Patterns

We express emotions with words: "I feel happy," "I'm scared," "I'm anxious," "I feel calm." But emotions, before they are words, flow through the brain like electricity. Right now, whatever emotion you're feeling—the emotion is being exchanged as electrical signals between neurons in the brain. These signals can be measured as brainwaves, and depending on the emotional state, they generate different frequencies. Our brain doesn't send a single signal. Depending on the emotion, it generates completely different rhythms and waveforms.

Emotions are not just "feelings." They are patterns that emerge from electrical currents. And that flow can be read by machines. The emotional design devices we encounter in daily life are all based on these brainwave rhythms. Horror-inducing videos raise gamma waves. Gamma waves activate short-term memory, so the emotions experienced during this time are the most likely to stay in memory. Horror games or disaster news stimulate gamma waves above 30Hz, simultaneously increasing heart rate and anxiety, making fear feel "real."

Meditation apps induce relaxation through alpha waves. Repetitive breathing guidance, natural sounds, and slow-tempo music induce alpha waves (8–12Hz). At that moment, people feel "calm," but in reality, their brainwaves are quietly being re-adjusted to the most stable rhythm.

BCI technology amplifies concentration or blurs willpower. When focus is needed, beta waves are amplified to increase decision-making and judgment. On the other hand, when theta waves are induced, concentration weakens, and ego boundaries become loosened. At this time, people feel "tired," "my thoughts are unclear," but in fact, the brainwaves have been induced into a state of avoiding decisions.

Before we feel emotions, electrical signals flow first. Emotions come before thought, and those emotions can be measured faster than the thought itself. When we say "technology reads emotions," it ultimately means it reads electrical signals. And if we can change the rhythm of that electrical flow, we can manipulate the structure of emotions.

Emotions are not language. They are not feelings. Emotions are waveforms, electrical flows. And right now, that flow is quietly being measured, quietly being designed, and sometimes quietly manipulated.

The Chemistry Behind Emotions

My mood might just be created by my hormones. We often explain emotions as electrical signals. But it's not just electricity that controls the speed, duration, and delicate texture of emotions.

The neurotransmitters and hormones that flow through our brain. They are like directors of emotions, making some feelings last longer and causing others to explode in an instant. And these chemical flows can be adjusted according to the environment, even without our conscious awareness. Sometimes, they can be deliberately designed.

Dopamine — The Emotion of Addiction and Repetition

When you open social media and receive a 'like' notification, a small joy passes through you. You scroll down to the next feed, and another response appears. At that moment, dopamine is released in your brain. Dopamine is the "reward prediction system." When you expect "another joy," it is released in anticipation.

Addiction begins when this "expected joy" is repeated. Emotional manipulation systems target this dopamine loop. Recommendation algorithms continue to feed "possibly interesting" content, and ads whisper "this is perfect for you." The brain reacts not to reality, but to the expectation, choosing repetition.

Serotonin — Designing the Message of Stability

A meditation app sends you a notification: "Finish your day with calm." You follow the voice, breathe along, and hear the phrase: "It's okay to live in the moment." Shortly after, your mind settles down. This sense of calm is due to serotonin's action. Serotonin helps maintain emotional balance and satisfaction. On the contrary, when serotonin levels drop, anxiety and impulsiveness increase.

Emotion-inducing content is designed to match serotonin release conditions. Lyrical language, repetitive rhythms, and warm colors—all these elements are set to induce serotonin responses. You feel "comfortable," but in reality, that comfort might be a response designed by structure.

Oxytocin — Designing Group Emotions of 'Empathy'

"You are not alone." "We are stronger together." In 2020, a social campaign used this message to create simultaneous empathy among people. In the comment section, responses like "I was moved" and "Why am I crying?" followed.

The key substance here is oxytocin. Oxytocin is the hormone that creates trust, bonding, and a sense of belonging. It is released when social contact and emotional connections to others' suffering are promoted.

Emotion designers target this "empathy circuit." Background music, emotional interviews, and images of children and the elderly—all visual and auditory stimuli are set to fulfill the conditions for oxytocin release. We feel "empathetic," but in reality, that emotion might be induced.

Cortisol — Designing the Emotion of Anxiety

"You didn't know this shocking truth." "Things are only going to get worse." "If you don't act now, it'll be too late." These are the typical phrases seen in online news headlines. They aren't just provocative sentences. They are designed to stimulate our stress system.

The substance released here is cortisol. Cortisol is the hormone that regulates long-term stress responses. With repeated exposure, it weakens the immune system and dulls emotional responses.

Some platforms use this "repeated exposure to crisis" to keep users engaged. News structures designed not to resolve anxiety, threatening messages that induce clicks, and emotional coercion that doesn't stop until you find an answer.

Emotions are chemicals. And chemicals can be designed.

Dopamine, serotonin, oxytocin, cortisol. The combinations and timing of these chemicals make us feel "happy," "anxious," or "at ease."

And technology now understands the conditions to induce these chemical reactions. Repetitive rhythms, specific word combinations, the structure of content, and the intensity of visuals and sounds—all these elements combine to create emotions we believe are "ours." But in reality, that emotion may have been planned. The feeling feels like it's ours, but the signals that created it were already given. Emotions are chemicals. And chemicals can be designed.

Judgment Comes After Emotion

What always moves first is emotion. We often believe we are rational and logical beings. We think we make decisions after sufficient thought and information review.

But neuroscientists tell a different story. We don't make decisions logically. Instead, emotion moves first, and then we bring logic to explain it. In other words, emotions reach the brain before judgment.

Even with the same event, we feel completely different emotions when we read these two sentences:

"Vaccination rates finally surpassed 80%!"

"Still 20% unvaccinated… the danger remains."

Both sentences deliver the same information, but one induces relief, while the other induces anxiety. We think we've "judged based on information," but in reality, emotions react first, and judgment follows based on that emotion. Anxiety soon impacts political stances, consumption choices, and behavioral patterns.

The moment emotion is shaken, judgment is shaken too. This is where BCI technology becomes dangerous. BCI doesn't directly "explain" emotions. Instead, it creates the conditions to let those emotions flow. Repetitive sounds with certain rhythms, user interfaces filled with emotional vocabulary, and content with "emotion-triggering sections." All of these stimuli lead, build, and adjust the flow of emotions. Then, later, when we say "This judgment was mine," it is likely that that judgment was the result of emotional flow.

Emotions → Judgment Structural Order

1. We receive a stimulus (news, images, tone, speed, etc.)
2. An emotional response happens first (brainwave + hormone reaction)
3. The brain starts searching for reasons for that emotion
4. Logic and judgment follow ("So I must do this.")

If the direction of emotion is manipulated, judgment and decision-making will be manipulated along with it.

The scariest thing about emotional manipulation is that we believe that judgment was "our own choice." BCI technology isn't about forcefully issuing commands to the brain. It's about shaking the flow of emotions first and letting judgment be built on top of that. As a result, we act, believe, and decide based on the flow of emotion, not information. "I felt this judgment was correct." But that "feeling" might have been designed by the emotional pathway that preceded it.

Emotions Are Easily Shaken

Emotions feel like something that arises naturally from deep inside us. Sometimes they are so intense that we can't explain them, and sometimes they are so subtle that we can hardly name them. We believe that they are natural experiences, and that they come from our instincts and intuition. But neuroscience and BCI technology say otherwise. Emotions are not abstract concepts; they are measurable.

Emotions are not just a fleeting feeling. They are patterns of electrical flows in the brain, waves created by hormones, and the direction of interpretations built by neural circuits. In other words, emotions are a reactive system with generating conditions. If this structure exists, it inherently includes the possibility of being designed.

If we subtly alter the pathway where emotions flow, if we repeatedly trigger the stimuli that induce emotions, if we twist the way memories and emotions connect, that emotion might seem like something I felt, but in reality, it could be an emotion designed by technology.

We believe that emotions are "natural internal flows," but we are living in an era where the possibility of designing and controlling them already exists. Without realizing it, we are increasingly living influenced by the flow of emotions.

Chapter 11. Our Minds Read Through Brainwaves, Skin, and Light

The Technologies Reading Emotions Today

The phrase "reading emotions" once sounded like a poetic metaphor—the ability to look into someone's eyes, feel the tremor in their expression, and sense their feelings without words. Such emotional intuition was considered rare and artistic. But today, the meaning of "reading emotions" has shifted completely. Science has turned it into a technological command.

Now, we can detect emotions in real time through brainwaves, skin conductivity, and blood flow—without speaking or shedding a tear. Even before you say you feel bad, your neurons are already firing, your heart is reacting, your brain's frequencies are adjusting, your palms are sweating, and your pupils are trembling. Today's technology detects these changes within seconds, quantifies them, and, if necessary, stores and categorizes them.

In this chapter, we explore how science reads emotions and how this reading paves the way for behavioral design. We focus on three core technologies:

- EEG: The oldest tool for reading brainwaves.
- GSR: The simplest sensory method for detecting emotional changes through the skin.
- fNIRS: A device using near-infrared light to locate where emotions arise in the brain.

Today, these technologies can map emotional landscapes as clearly as drawing a map on paper. And on that map, decisions are being made about which emotions to amplify and which to suppress.

EEG: The Oldest Window into Emotion

Electroencephalography, or EEG, is often the first technology people encounter in the field of emotional reading. By attaching electrodes to the scalp, EEG detects tiny electrical signals produced by neurons, allowing researchers to monitor which parts of the brain are active in real time. Crucially, EEG can capture emotional activity even before you consciously recognize it.

Example: How Ads Design Emotional Flow

In 2019, a global sports brand conducted an EEG-based immersion experiment with 300 consumers to design an emotional arc for a new ad campaign. The surprising result?

- The strongest emotional spike did not occur when the brand logo appeared.
- Instead, it happened during a 3-second scene where an athlete collapsed and gasped for breath.

The ad was re-edited to focus on "endurance" rather than "victory," creating a much stronger emotional impact. However, this impact wasn't natural; it was calculated through EEG data.

Example: Is a Horror Game Really Scary?

Before launching a psychological horror game, a game company used EEG to measure brain responses. Surprisingly, players' strongest reactions came not from jump scares, but from faint sounds in tense silence. The developers adjusted sound frequencies, lighting, and ambient noise based on these real-time brainwave readings. Ultimately, the "fear" players felt was the result of careful emotional engineering.

EEG today is not just for marketing. It's central to diagnosing and treating emotional disorders. For instance, depression patients show asymmetry in frontal alpha waves, and PTSD patients exhibit surges in beta and gamma waves. EEG can reveal not only emotional states but also how emotions are distorted or over-amplified. Its greatest power lies in capturing emotions before they are spoken, recognized, or even fully felt.

GSR: Capturing the Moment Emotions Erupt

Before words form or faces change, emotions first appear through the skin. Galvanic Skin Response (GSR) measures the electrical changes in your skin triggered by emotional arousal.

Why the skin? When we are emotionally stirred, heart rates quicken, body temperature rises slightly, and sweat glands activate—raising the skin's electrical conductivity. GSR picks up these tiny shifts, capturing the exact moment emotions begin.

Example: How GSR Predicted Purchasing Behavior

A major retailer conducted an experiment tracking GSR responses while customers walked through a store. Interestingly, the areas where customers had the strongest emotional reactions—not where they lingered the longest—showed the highest purchase conversion rates.

It wasn't hesitation that led to buying—it was emotional spikes. Based on this data, product displays were reorganized according to GSR readings, and both customer satisfaction and sales improved.

GSR doesn't interpret why you're anxious or happy. It simply pinpoints when your emotional response ignites—and sometimes, that's all a system needs to influence behavior without needing to know anything else.

fNIRS: Light That Illuminates the Beginning of Emotions

While emotions often feel like they arise in the heart, they are actually orchestrated by multiple brain regions. Functional Near-Infrared Spectroscopy (fNIRS) is a technology that shines light on this hidden landscape by tracking blood flow to emotional processing areas.

When you feel an emotion, blood rushes to certain parts of your brain. Emotions consume energy, and fNIRS detects these shifts in oxygenated blood, helping locate where emotions originate.

Example: Tracking Genuine Joy

In 2022, an AI startup conducted an fNIRS experiment to track genuine joy.

- Personalized video clips were shown, and brain activity was recorded.
- True joy consistently activated the left prefrontal cortex, while socially forced laughter showed stronger amygdala activation, signaling discomfort.

This study revealed that fNIRS can not only detect when emotions occur but also distinguish real emotional experiences from artificial ones.

Example: Predicting Depression Treatment Responses

A university hospital used fNIRS to predict how patients would respond to antidepressants.

- Some patients showed minimal prefrontal cortex activation even when exposed to positive stimuli.
- Others displayed excessive negative responses in the amygdala.

Based on these brain patterns, treatment plans were better tailored, improving success rates compared to traditional symptom-based diagnosis.

Today, emotions are no longer invisible, private experiences. They are measurable, locatable, and increasingly predictable.

When joy flares in your brain, oxygen floods to a specific region—and technology can now detect, record, and analyze it.

Once the birthplace of emotions becomes visible, it becomes manipulatable. That is the reality we must now recognize.

Chapter 12. Your Emotions Are Being Called

How Emotional Flows Are Engineered

We tend to accept emotions as natural phenomena. They rise at the right moment, surge without clear reason, and we often believe that emotions are "real" precisely because they feel inexplicable.

However, technology views emotions very differently. It doesn't ask, "Why do you feel this way?" Instead, it calculates, "When we give this stimulus, what reaction will appear after a few seconds?" That reaction becomes a pattern, a probability, a repeatable condition within the machine's language.

Emotions are no longer something that must patiently emerge. Technology can now *create* emotions. Whether the feelings are truly yours, or whether they are even genuine, no longer matters. What matters is whether your brain reacted, whether your skin conducted electricity, whether blood flowed to a certain area. If it did, the machine records it: the emotion was induced.

We may believe we "felt" the emotion. But the machine would say: "We flowed it." And so the question becomes: Did I really choose this feeling, or was it something that simply passed through me—designed by someone else? Now, we must face the stimuli and technology that quietly shape our emotions.

Invisible Manipulation Through Electromagnetic Waves
People often think that to manipulate the brain, something must be inserted—surgery, implants, or invasive procedures. But emotional manipulation today works without even touching the brain. Before you even notice, your emotions may already have been adjusted.

tDCS: Changing Emotions with Electric Current
Transcranial Direct Current Stimulation (tDCS) is a

headband-like device that sends a weak direct current across the scalp. You don't feel it. But your brain cells do. In an American neuroscience lab, participants solved ethical dilemmas after receiving tDCS stimulation on the left prefrontal cortex. The result? Participants made more utilitarian choices—willing to sacrifice one to save many—far more often than before. They believed they were "thinking logically," but in truth, their thinking had been silently nudged.

TMS: Switching Emotional Circuits On and Off

Transcranial Magnetic Stimulation (TMS) uses strong magnetic pulses targeted to the brain. In a German study, TMS temporarily disconnected the amygdala from the prefrontal cortex. Suddenly, participants could no longer regulate emotions properly. Even small triggers caused overwhelming anxiety.

This experiment shows that if technology can calm emotions, it can also trigger emotional overload. The emotional circuit is no longer sacred—it can be manipulated.

RF: Undetectable, Yet Invasive

Radio Frequency (RF) stimulation, considered one of the

most concerning technologies, uses low-intensity radio waves. No one feels it, hears it, or sees it. But over time, RF stimulation can induce overactivity in fear, vigilance, insomnia, and irritability circuits.

In a military experiment, soldiers exposed to RF reported loss of concentration, mood swings, insomnia, and chronic fatigue. They weren't plugged into anything. They didn't hear a sound. Yet, their emotions were disturbed.

- tDCS adjusts thoughts.
- TMS turns emotional circuits on and off.
- RF quietly shakes emotions from the shadows.

These technologies don't persuade with logic. They lightly touch the emotional flow itself—changing judgments, choices, and even identity—without a word or touch.

Visual Stimuli: Images That Create Emotions

We think we're just seeing images. But we're actually feeling through them.

Vision is the fastest, deepest emotional sense. Sound passes through the ear, but images directly stimulate the brain's visual cortex, connected tightly to emotional circuits. And these emotional responses can be meticulously designed.

Example: Political Ads Adjusting Judgments Through Color

In the 2020 election, two candidates had almost identical policies. Yet voters reacted differently because of color and editing.

- Candidate A: Blue background, slow zoom, gentle music.
- Candidate B: Red background, rapid cuts, sharp contrasts.

Even though the words were the same, Candidate B was perceived as more aggressive and threatening.

The content hadn't changed—only the colors and rhythms had. Yet emotional impressions, and thus judgment, shifted dramatically.

Example: Editing Refugee Documentaries to Induce Sympathy

A human rights documentary initially failed to emotionally engage viewers. So producers re-edited: lowering lighting, switching to black-and-white, slowing crying scenes, and adding soft piano music.

Suddenly, audiences said: "I teared up," "I felt their pain." It wasn't the refugees' stories that changed—it was the structure of visual and auditory stimuli.

Editing Rhythms Shape Emotions

- Fast cuts (<1 sec): heighten anxiety and heart rate.
- Long takes (5+ sec) with slow zoom: build immersion and emotional identification.
- Close-ups every 3 seconds: induce empathy and trust.

Same content, different design—entirely different emotional experiences.

Emotions are not born from *what* you see, but *how* you see it.

Language Triggers: Hidden Emotional Codes

Language doesn't just convey emotions—it now *triggers* them.

Copywriting used to rely on intuition. Today, emotional reactions to sentence structures are calculated, predicted, and designed.

Example: Headlines That Induce Anxiety

Two headlines delivering the same message:

- A: "Interest rates expected to rise next year."

- B: "If you delay, your loan may become risky."

Headline B got 2.4x more clicks.

Words like "delay," "risk," and "your loan" trigger cortisol responses—activating anxiety.

Example: Designing Responsibility in Campaign Messages

Blood donation A/B test:

- A: "Blood donation saves lives. Please participate."
- B: "Your blood is needed now. Only you can save lives."

Version B tripled the response rate.

Urgency ("now") and personal responsibility ("only you") activated a strong oxytocin and guilt response, driving action through emotion.

Example: Sermons and Speeches—Why They Sound the Same

Whether in politics or religion, the formulas are strikingly similar:

- "We are one."
- "We must act now."
- "Silence is complicity."

These phrases are not random—they are emotionally engineered structures.

Emotion is triggered before understanding. Language now shapes emotional pathways faster than reason can catch up.

Emotions Being Called

Once, emotions arose naturally. They came with love, sadness, joy, anger—when we were ready.

Now, they no longer wait.

Technology knows what triggers emotions and holds the architecture to summon them.

A small surge of electricity. A flash of an image. A single carefully crafted phrase.

That's all it takes to lead emotions down a predesigned path.

The emotions are real. You really cried. You really got angry. You really felt moved.

But now, we must ask: "Why here?", "Why now?", "Why this feeling?"

The power to ask those questions—before simply riding the emotional wave—is the true power we must now reclaim.

Chapter 13. The Era of Storing Memories Externally

Memories Can Be Stored

For a long time, we believed memories were ours. They were our past, the foundation of our emotions, and the basis of every choice we made. Memories were not just records—they were the deepest foundation of who we are. What have I experienced? What have I felt? What choices have I made? These questions were woven into the memories that shaped our identity.

But today, memories are being read, stored, and even restored. They are quietly becoming data—something that can be manipulated. Brainwave-reading technologies have made it possible to capture the electrical signals that form memories and convert them into digital codes. Those codes are no longer confined within us. They can now be stored externally—on devices, servers, and invisible digital flows. We now face new, unsettling questions. If my memories define who I am, can I still be "me" when those memories have been manipulated? If memories can be modified, could emotions, beliefs, and even my very sense of self be altered too? Memories were once considered the inevitable traces of our past, subject to fading but fundamentally authentic. But now, they are shifting toward something entirely different—something editable, transferable, and programmable.

Neurons fire patterns to recall a memory. That subtle electrical flow says, "I was there." Technologies like Neuralink are beginning to read these flows, turning neuron activity into digital codes. In a world where memories are uploaded to cloud servers and retrieved at will, memories no longer fade. They persist. But another question follows: when memories become data, are they still truly mine? As we move into this new reality, the very concept of memory—and therefore identity—is being redefined.

Memory Backup: The Task of Cloning Myself

Neuralink's ambition isn't just to read brainwaves. Elon Musk envisions a world where "Memories can be stored like files and retrieved whenever we want." Imagine a man vividly remembering a warm summer day at the beach, only to have that memory blur over time—the sound of the waves, the scent of the ocean, the feel of pebbles slipping from his hand.

Now imagine if that memory had been stored digitally, as neuron firing patterns. And someday, it could be reinserted back into his brain. He could relive that day exactly as it was—the warmth, the light, the sound. Memory backup offers more than preservation. It suggests the possibility of cloning identity itself. If entire sets of memories could be copied and implanted into another body or machine, would the person who emerges still be "me"? Or just someone who resembles me?

Memory backup isn't just a technological innovation. It's a door opening onto the possibility of duplicating, replicating, and ultimately redesigning what it means to exist. If my memories are cloned, can I still claim to be unique? The lines between selfhood and replication are beginning to blur.

Erasing and Planting Memories

Memory technology no longer just preserves—it can alter. Research is now underway to erase traumatic memories by weakening the neural patterns that encode them, or by blocking the emotional circuits that give them force. PTSD therapies are already attempting to diminish the pain associated with traumatic flashbacks, making those memories lose their emotional sting.

Other studies aim to restore fading memories. In Alzheimer's experiments, electrical stimulation is used to strengthen neural connections, reviving memories of childhood, family, and lost moments. Even more astonishing is the possibility of implanting memories that never existed. Experiments have shown that specific combinations of visual and auditory stimuli can convince people they remember events that never occurred. *"I lost my balloon at the amusement park,"* someone might say, even though no such event ever happened.

The brain, especially when emotions are involved, sometimes cannot distinguish between real and constructed memories. And if memories define our sense of self, what happens when those memories can be fabricated? Memory modification holds promise for healing—but it also quietly shakes the very foundation of human existence.

What Collapses When Memories Are Distorted

Memories aren't just recollections of the past. They are emotional triggers. When memories resurface, they stir joy, anger, sorrow, or hope. Emotions drive judgments. Judgments drive actions. And actions, over time, shape belief systems and identities.

Imagine a woman whose memory of walking hand-in-hand with her grandmother in a sunlit park has long been her emotional anchor. That memory whispers: "You were loved." "You matter." It supports her choices, her relationships, her resilience. But if that memory were erased—or worse, replaced with a memory of abandonment—her entire emotional structure would collapse. Love would seem dangerous. Trust would wither. Self-worth would crumble.

Memory manipulation is not just about changing a few mental images. It can twist emotions, warp decisions, and rewrite entire life narratives. If our memories can be edited like files, then our emotions, choices, and sense of agency become fragile too. Once again, the question returns: Who am I, if my memories can change?

The Edge Between Memory and Free Will

We believe we are the sum of our memories. "My experiences and emotions made me who I am." But if memories can be stored externally, modified, or even fabricated, then can we still call ourselves truly "ourselves"?

Imagine a young man who grew up trusting others, smiling easily, and believing in kindness. His memories are filled with playground laughter, family warmth, and moments of pride. But one day, someone alters his memories—deleting the warmth, emphasizing rejection.

The physical world hasn't changed. But the world he remembers has. Now, he distrusts easily, carries quiet anger, and withdraws. He feels he has changed—but doesn't realize that what truly changed were his memories.

When memories change, emotions change.

When emotions change, choices change.

When choices change, free will itself is threatened.

Are we truly making free choices? Or are we simply walking down paths laid by manipulated memories?

Neuralink and other technologies dream of a future where memories can be backed up, downloaded, edited. In that future, we must ask urgently: If my memories can be altered, can I still call my choices free?

When memories become external data—and when that data can be rewritten—free will may no longer be an act of a pure, autonomous mind. At that moment, the very definition of humanity may shift into something we do not yet fully understand.

Chapter 14: Did I Really Choose This?

Pre-designed Choices

You read the news in the morning, order something for lunch, and pick a movie to watch in the evening. In each of those moments, you feel like you made the decision for yourself. But did you really? The article you clicked on, the product you chose, the sentence and image you were drawn to—could they have been pre-arranged emotional choices? Choices cannot exist without options. And now, technology is focused on how to present those 'options': which words to show first, which buttons to enlarge, which emotions to trigger first so that the "right" choice naturally follows. Technology no longer directly forces how you decide. Instead, it quietly designs what you are able to choose.

Decisions Are Guided Within the Flow

We make dozens of decisions every day—what to click, what to eat, what expression to wear. All of these decisions seem quick or casual. But in reality, they happen within a carefully connected flow of emotions, cognition, and context. That flow moves in order: an emotional reaction occurs first, logic is constructed afterward to justify that feeling, and then we select the option that feels "just a little better." Decision-making is not pure calculation—it is a flow. And crucially, this flow can be calculated and influenced.

For example, an electric car brand offered a simple table comparing three models. The premium model was placed on the left, the basic model on the right, and the "Standard Plus" model—slightly upgraded yet far cheaper than the premium—was placed at the center, where attention naturally gravitates. A small note read: "The most popular choice." This design alone shifted decision patterns dramatically. Most users chose the center model, not necessarily because it was the best objectively, but because it felt emotionally safest. Technology does not attack your reason. It softly guides your emotional flow.

We believe we make rational choices. But often, by the time we choose, the options have already been emotionally tilted. The colors, layouts, wording, spacing—everything is subtly tuned to nudge our emotions toward a specific choice. In the end, what we call "decision-making" might just be the next reaction along a pre-designed emotional flow.

Psychological Framing: Different Judgments from Same Facts

We like to think that we judge information objectively— evaluating facts, numbers, and logic. But framing determines how that information emotionally reaches us. The same facts, wrapped in different emotional tones, lead to completely different judgments.

Consider two headlines for the same product:

• "90% of customers were satisfied."

• "10% of customers were dissatisfied."

The information is identical. But the emotional reaction is not. Readers of the first headline feel safer. Those who see the second feel wary. Brain imaging studies show stronger fear-related brain activity in the latter case, leading to hesitation and avoidance. It's not logic that changes. It's the emotional starting point that shifts the judgment.

The same phenomenon occurs in politics. A neutral headline like "Candidate X is reviewing a new bill" has far less emotional pull than "Candidate X insists the bill protecting citizens must be passed now." Though quoting the same interview, the emotional urgency changes impressions dramatically. Framing doesn't lie. It selects which emotional reaction will accompany the information. We believe we see the world objectively. But most information we receive comes pre-wrapped—shaped to evoke specific emotions before we even consciously process it.

How Emotion Shapes Decisions

Emotional design doesn't force you to decide. Instead, it starts your emotions flowing, and your judgments quietly follow. Because the process is soft and seamless, you don't notice the emotional path you are following.

In an online education platform, a particular course was designed to stand out with a dark background, subtle animations, and a slight zoom-in effect. Other courses were muted and static. Users said, "It just caught my eye." In reality, attention was carefully guided. Options weren't removed. The visibility of options was tilted.

Similarly, during limited-time sales events, shopping sites use countdown timers, scarcity warnings like "Only 3 left!", and urgent messages like "Buy before it's too late." Users don't deliberate for long. Excitement and anxiety quicken decisions. The average time spent on the page drops, but purchase rates spike.

Logic can explain a judgment afterward. But emotions decide first:

• Focus reduces awareness of alternatives.

• Guilt accelerates action.

• Excitement speeds up judgment before doubt can intervene.

These emotional triggers are engineered. They make you feel you made a decision yourself. But before you even reached the fork in the road, emotions had already begun flowing toward a pre-arranged outcome.

The Disguised Freedom of Choices

We make choices constantly—what to read, what to buy, whom to trust. These small decisions, compounded over time, shape who we are and the society we inhabit. Thus, we fiercely want to believe: "I thought carefully and chose freely."

But the truth is, emotions always move first. Technology designs where those emotions begin, how they flow, and which options feel more "right." Every color, every word, every button position is engineered to quietly steer your emotional current.

Judgment feels like freedom. But if that freedom only moves along an emotional river already dug for us, can it still be called freedom? Or is it a beautifully disguised reaction?

We feel like we made the decision. But the path—the colors, the emotions, the choices offered—was already laid down for us. To claim our choices as truly ours, we must first learn to see the hidden flow guiding them.

Only when we can read that emotional river can we truly reclaim the freedom to choose.

Part 4.

Safeguarding Your

Feelings in a Digital Age

Chapter 15: My Emotions, My Memories... Who Will Protect Them?

Who Guards the "Me" I Remember?

Memory is me. Emotion is me. Judgment is me. For a long time, we have defined ourselves in this way: "What I feel, what I judge, and what I remember is who I am." But today, when all of these can be measured, manipulated, and imposed by technology, can we still say, "I am truly myself"? Technology now has the power to induce emotions, distort judgments, reorder memories, and selectively highlight or erase them. EEG reads emotions, TMS stimulates decision circuits, and language triggers guide memories in specific directions. Machines stir emotions before we are even aware, rearrange memories before we realize, and emotionally arrange choices before we decide.

As technology grows, so must the boundaries that protect human identity. It begins with a new declaration: to protect emotions and memories as integral rights of being human.

Emotions, Judgments, Memories: The Three Targets

The deepest assets that form who we are can be traced to three elements: emotion determines how we perceive the world, judgment reveals the kind of choices we make, and memory ties our past to our present. These three are inseparable. We judge in the flow of emotions, we feel through memory, and we find ourselves within these interactions.

Now, technology is accessing these domains more skillfully and silently than ever before. Memory is no longer merely internal—it becomes a stored experience, often entangled with emotional reactions. Some memories warm us, some tighten our bodies, and others replay themselves, destabilizing our present.

The core of memory is not just the content but the emotional echo it brings. What if technology could erase that emotional resonance? If the memory remains but no longer triggers any feeling, can we still call it "our memory"? In experiments treating PTSD with TMS, soldiers' memories of trauma remained intact, but their emotional responses were dulled. "I remember the event," they said, "but it no longer affects me." Therapeutically, this may help. But it also foreshadows something darker: the transformation of memory into neutral data, stripped of lived significance.

If memory can be dulled until it no longer demands acknowledgment, no longer stirs action—then technology has not healed, but invaded. Memory is alive only when it is felt.

What Should 'Human Rights' Be?

Emotion, judgment, memory—these must now be recognized not just as private experiences, but as rights. Technology has already breached the inner realms of humanity, often without any formal recognition.

We must now ask: Are emotions assets to be protected? Should memories carry legal rights? Should consciousness itself be shielded as an inviolable space?

In 2022, a global e-commerce platform designed advertising algorithms that read users' emotional flows. Users under emotional fatigue were targeted with "urgent discount" offers, resulting in impulsive purchases. Later, many wondered, "Why did I buy that?" Was that feeling theirs, or a cleverly triggered manipulation?

In 2021, a digital therapy startup tested "emotion reconstruction algorithms," repeatedly exposing users to messages like, "It wasn't your fault," or "You did your best." Participants eventually reported that painful memories now felt "insignificant," or like "just a scene." Memories weren't erased—but the emotional and moral tones were subtly altered. Experiences once deemed traumatic became softened, neutralized, reinterpreted. Memory is not just raw information. It derives meaning from the emotions it carries. When emotion is reconstructed, meaning is reconstructed. And when meaning is altered, human dignity itself is threatened.

Why Memory and Consciousness Must Be Protected
Memory is not simply data—it is living proof of our journey through life. We define ourselves through

memories: what we have seen, felt, and chosen. Every memory contains tears we shed, nights we couldn't forgive, mornings when we chose to trust again.

Now, memory is becoming technological territory. Emotional responses are categorized, memories are analyzed, and some are suppressed while others are amplified. Technology does not delete memories outright. Instead, it controls how we feel about them—and in doing so, rewrites what those memories mean.

We must ask:

• Is the "me" I remember truly mine?

• Can I still claim ownership of a memory whose emotional tone has been altered?

This is no longer a matter of philosophical anxiety. It is a practical question of survival in a digital era. Emotions, memory, consciousness—these must now be recognized as protected rights.

Technology will not stop. Therefore, humanity must establish new rights: the right to protect memory, the right to safeguard emotions, and the right to defend consciousness against unauthorized intrusion. Memory is the scaffold that holds together the timeline of our lives.

Emotion is the energy that keeps memory alive.

Consciousness is the final center that binds it all together as "me."

We must defend this structure. It is the last, and most sacred, boundary between human beings and technology's reach.

Chapter 16: The Rise of Brain Sovereignty

An Era Where Even Thoughts Aren't Safe

For a long time, emotion was seen as the proof of humanity—something machines could never fully replicate, something beyond logic and language. Yet today, emotions are increasingly being treated as data. Technology reads them as measurable signals, sorts them into predictable patterns, and converts them into stimuli that can be induced and controlled.

Advertising algorithms convert your emotions into click-through rates. Political messages calculate which sentences stir feelings the fastest. Treatment machines quietly define "normal emotional ranges," cutting off what they label "excessive." Brainwave sensors read your state before you even speak.

Technology says: "We can read your emotions. We can measure your brainwaves and guide your judgment." But we must ask: "If my emotions can be read and guided, are they still truly mine?" Technology doesn't scream or force; it just quietly seeps in under the guise of "understanding." And that's exactly where the danger lies—when the tool for understanding becomes a weapon for control.

One day, you may wonder: "Is this emotion really mine?" "Why does this memory feel so distant?" "Why does this judgment feel as if it wasn't fully mine?" At that moment, we must realize: technology has already begun to quietly cross the sacred boundary of human identity.

Emotion Is Not Data

Emotion is not a number. Emotion is the raw pulse of existence. It is the unseen frequency through which humans meet the world, interpret it, and respond to it. Sadness signals what we have lost. Anger points us to what we must protect. Joy reveals where we belong. Emotion shows us how our life is stitched together.

But technology has started to see emotion differently—as something measurable, sortable, and monetizable. Sadness becomes stress level. Joy becomes a consumer reaction. Anxiety becomes a risk profile. Emotions are reduced to engagement metrics, ad-click probabilities, user behavior predictions. In that process, emotion becomes a tool—no longer a free internal experience, but an external asset to be harvested.

One global streaming service analyzed users' emotional curves in real time—adjusting recommendations, colors, pacing, narration based on viewers' moods. It wasn't offering comfort; it was placing your emotions into a funnel for commerce. Another mental health app turned daily feelings into numerical codes—0 for indifference, 1 for mild depression, 2 for moderate anxiety. Users began to see their own emotions through these codes, treating their inner world like a status report.

Emotion can be measured, yes. But it should never be compressed, managed, or commodified. Emotion is interpretation. It's the lens through which I meet the world. Once others start interpreting my emotions for me, I lose ownership of my own being.

Emotions Are Sacred Personal Domains

Even if emotion can be measured, it must not be designed. Emotion is mine. It is tied to judgment, to memory, and to the construction of identity itself. The moment technology crosses into this space, we must draw a clear line and declare: emotional sovereignty.

In 2020, a political campaign secretly conducted a BCI emotional measurement project. Emotional peaks—anger, empathy, anxiety—were precisely tracked and engineered into speeches and advertisements. Voters believed they had decided freely. In reality, their emotions had already been meticulously channeled.

A global company ran EEG and GSR-based tests during an ad launch. Consumers cried, bought, believed—feeling it was real, while unaware their emotional landscape had been quietly mapped and manipulated.

Was the emotion real? Yes. But was the path that led to it natural? No. This is the difference. It's not about whether the feeling is genuine. It's about whether the feeling was summoned by you—or designed for you.

Emotion is not data. Emotion is dignity. And no technology, however advanced, has the right to interpret or manipulate it without profound respect and explicit consent.

What Is Neurosovereignty?

Neurosovereignty is the right to control your own brain— your thoughts, emotions, memories, and decisions—free from unwanted measurement or manipulation. In the past, human rights protected physical autonomy. Now, they must also protect mental autonomy.

In 2022, a global beauty brand tested emotional reactions during product trials using EEG data. Based on brainwave responses, they altered package designs and marketing phrases. One participant later said, "I started wondering: Did I actually feel that way, or was I just nudged into believing I did?"

An AI-driven mental health platform tailored counseling messages based on users' brainwave patterns. At first, it felt reassuring. Over time, users noticed: "No matter what I felt, the platform responded in the same way." Emotional individuality was flattened, responses pre-scripted. If your emotion is detected before you express it, if your content is suggested before you choose it, then you slowly lose the ability to feel and act for yourself.

The proof that the brain belongs to me lies in my freedom to feel and decide. If brainwaves are monitored, emotions pre-empted, and decisions silently nudged, then humanity itself is at stake. And at that moment, we must have the courage to say, "This is wrong."

Neurosovereignty isn't about resisting machines altogether. It's about preserving the space to feel, remember, judge— alone and authentically.

Emotion Is the Deepest Freedom

Emotion is not data to be collected or optimized. Emotion is born where the human spirit touches the world. It can't be predicted. It doesn't need to be explained. It doesn't have to make sense. Sometimes it's illogical—and yet profoundly true.

Today, technology tracks every emotional signal. It designs purchases, calibrates ads, shapes political views, and molds social reactions—all based on those signals. This manipulation is hidden under the name of "personalization." But we must ask: is an optimized emotion truly my emotion?

If emotion is not protected, memory cannot be protected. If memory falls, judgment falls. And if judgment falls, so does free will. To preserve human dignity, we must protect emotions first.

Emotion is the final untouched freedom at the core of human life. It is the last sovereignty that technology must not cross. It is the new frontier for human rights. And it is the most silent, yet most fiercely important freedom we must defend.

Chapter 17: Manipulated Emotions Aren't Mental Illness

The Quiet Collapse of the Self

The fact that technology can intervene in emotions is no longer strange. A world where emotions are designed, memories edited, and judgments quietly guided—this is the structure we have already explored in previous chapters. But now, let's look at a different scene: the people who are truly crumbling within this system, and the quiet, devastating suffering they are experiencing.

In an era where technology can manipulate emotions, pain also evolves. It is no longer visible wounds. It sounds like this: "My emotions don't feel like my own." "The way I feel myself seems unfamiliar." Something feels undeniably wrong, different from how one usually feels, yet no one believes it. This suffering is not mere discomfort; it is a quiet collapse of the inner self—the unsettling sensation that "something inside me has shifted."

The problem is that technology leaves no traces. The manipulation of emotions does not show up anywhere. The person's claims are unverifiable. Eventually, society labels this kind of pain as "mental illness." At this moment, the most devastating misunderstanding occurs: those whose emotions are distorted are not seen as victims of technological interference, but as people with pathology.

Victims Misdiagnosed as Mentally Ill

"This wasn't my real emotion. But the moment I said that, I became the 'strange one.'"

Those who have experienced technological manipulation of their emotions know it intimately. They know that the emotion is not natural. It feels as if it was "inserted"—an emotion that wasn't born inside but placed upon them. They say, "This isn't the emotion I normally feel," "Thoughts started forming, but they weren't mine," "Certain phrases or sounds cause sudden emotional surges."

These statements vividly describe the experience. Yet when presented to the medical system, they are reinterpreted. What is technological manipulation is mistaken for symptoms of mental illness.

Jeong-ah (pseudonym) began experiencing intense emotional surges while reading news captions in 2022. "It was just a passing headline, but suddenly my body froze, and I cried. The scene wouldn't leave my mind. Normally, I would have brushed it off." She initially suspected depression. But she was certain: "It wasn't depression. It wasn't my emotion. It felt like some signal had entered me." She sought help at a psychiatric clinic. But the diagnosis she received included mood disorder tendencies, early psychosis warnings, and derealization syndrome. She was prescribed medication. And all she could feel was: "The moment I said my emotions were manipulated, I became a patient."

The Boundary Between Emotional Manipulation and Mental Illness

Those whose emotional flow is disrupted by technology can sharply distinguish the intrusion. They don't fail to explain it—they explain it too precisely. They feel an unmistakable alienation: "This emotion isn't mine."

Unlike mental illness, emotional insertion happens while maintaining self-awareness. This distinction is crucial.

Yun-jae (pseudonym), a mid-thirties office worker, had no psychological history. Yet one day, he began to feel that his emotions moved ahead of him. "I didn't want to be angry, but I got angry. I wasn't sad, but tears came." The emotions felt "pre-triggered," foreign. Specific words and captions triggered sudden emotional waves. He explained carefully at a clinic: "My emotions feel detached. They arise before I can process them." But the medical system diagnosed him with emotional dysregulation and early psychotic tendencies.

Thus, his heightened sensitivity—his very ability to distinguish his own emotional flow—was pathologized. Inside, he was quietly crumbling. And outside, no language existed to name his pain.

Technology Erases the Crime, Leaves the Pain

The tragedy is that technology leaves no fingerprints, only pain. The emotional manipulation is erased in the system. The person is left alone to carry the blame.

Brainwaves are read in real time but leave no external record. Emotional stimuli are hidden in ordinary language, colors, rhythms. Judgment flows are subtly guided, making choices seem self-directed.

Ultimately, all the victim can say is: "Something is wrong. This emotion isn't mine." But without a structural language to explain it, society labels them "unstable."

Current diagnostic tools—EEG, fMRI—don't track emotional flow. So strange emotions are interpreted as psychological vulnerability. Efforts to explain emotional changes are seen as cognitive distortions.

The possibility of technological intervention is never even raised. Diagnostic categories don't account for artificially induced emotional flows. As a result, the emotional traces left by technology are quietly erased. The victim's pain is classified under "mental illness"—a misdiagnosis caused by the absence of an appropriate language.

This Is a Crossing of the Line

Strange emotional flows do exist. Specific stimuli, repeated phrases, subtle rhythms—all induce real but artificial emotional shifts. However, because these manipulations are hidden within systems, victims are left without any visible proof.

Thus, the altered emotions are not recognized as evidence of infringement—but simply labeled as mental aberrations. Technology shook their emotions. But this manipulation is absent from medical records. It is absent from legal discussions. Ultimately, responsibility falls on the person who felt the pain, not on the technology that caused it.

We urgently need a new language—a language that can explain emotional manipulation. Otherwise, those quietly suffering will continue to be misunderstood.

If emotional destabilization is due to external technological intervention, it is not pathology—it is the trace of violated rights.

Society must now learn to listen when someone says, "This doesn't feel like me." It must recognize that "this isn't my emotion" is not a delusion, but an awareness of violation.

A new diagnostic category must be created to name the pain caused by technology. And human rights must evolve to protect the emotional sovereignty of individuals. Technology has already crossed into the realm of emotion. Instead of labeling the damage as illness, we must first read what the damaged emotions are trying to protect. Emotion itself is not broken. Emotion is being invaded. Only when we socially and institutionally acknowledge this can we open a new era of protecting humanity in the digital age.

Chapter 18: Unprotected Emotions, The Beginning of Legislation

Current Laws Can't Stop Emotional Invasion

For a long time, the laws we upheld responded quickly to physical threats, visible violence, and information left behind as clear traces. But the emotional invasions happening today leave no visible marks. Brainwaves disappear in real time, emotional stimuli dissolve into everyday language and images, and manipulated judgments seem like "voluntary choices." As a result, today's legal frameworks remain silent, leaving emotions unprotected with the assumption: "If you can't see it, it doesn't exist." The problem is clear. No one can be held responsible for manipulating emotional flows. Even if emotions are deliberately shaken, even if specific decisions are emotionally guided, even if the link between memory and emotion is subtly severed—there is no law recognizing it as a violation. Even when victims speak up, there are no legal protections to shield them.

Now that technology can measure emotions, guide emotional flows, and design judgments, we must ask: can we legislate to protect emotions? If my emotional flow has been violated, how can I seek protection? If my emotions have been measured and manipulated without my consent, who can be punished?

The biggest barrier is "intangibility." Current laws, including in South Korea, work well when something tangible has been harmed—a physical injury, leaked personal information, direct verbal threats. But emotional invasions are invisible. They leave no physical damage. Crucially, "emotions" themselves do not even exist within the framework of the law.

Thus, even when emotions are violated, no standard exists to acknowledge it as an "action." Victims are left without language or recognition. And so, we urgently need new legislation. Emotions must be legally protected. Emotional manipulation must be legally recognized. Human existence is expressed most purely through emotions—and if technology can now shake those emotions, then it is shaking human dignity itself.

How Legal Protection Would Change the Landscape

Min-su (pseudonym) realized he was subtly guided by emotional flow while shopping on a social media platform. Initially, he thought it was a simple recommendation system. But in reality, the platform was analyzing his facial expressions, gaze direction, and reaction speed in real time to prioritize "emotionally reactive products." Min-su considered legal action, feeling he had been nudged into purchases he wouldn't have otherwise made. Yet his lawyer replied: "I understand, but under current law, 'emotional flow' is not a protected right."

Right now, emotional invasion is intangible, and so it is denied. But if emotional protection laws were established, this pain would be given a name. Language would emerge, procedures would be created, and rights would be granted. Imagine the change:

- Victims would no longer have to "prove" their emotional violation through logical arguments.
- Saying, "My emotions feel strange," would trigger an investigation.
- Emotional flow disturbances would be officially recorded.
- Technology providers would bear the burden of proving non-intervention.

Until now, victims had to carry the burden of proof, isolated and powerless. But with legal protection, the responsibility shifts to the technology companies.

Furthermore, companies would have to approach emotions cautiously:

- Emotional data collection would require explicit consent.
- Emotion-driven recommendations would have to be transparently disclosed.
- All emotionally manipulative technologies would be subject to record-keeping.
- If emotional manipulation occurred, companies would face legal liability.

Emotions would no longer be hidden tools for profit. They would become protected aspects of human identity.

Countries Leading the Way

Institutions, not individuals, were the first to recognize the risk of emotional manipulation. Since 2018, organizations like the European Union, the U.S. Senate, and the United Nations have all begun to acknowledge that "emotions are human rights."

European Union:

The EU's GDPR in 2018 classified emotion-related data as sensitive information:

- Cannot collect or process emotional data without explicit consent.
- Bans emotion-based profiling.
- Requires companies to disclose purposes, methods, and retention periods for emotional data.

In Europe, you cannot even access emotional data without permission. Emotions have been officially recognized as part of human dignity.

United States:

Although the U.S. lacks a comprehensive law like the

GDPR, in 2022, the Senate proposed the Emotion AI Regulation Act:

- Requires disclosure of emotion-analysis algorithms.
- Mandatory notice for potential emotional manipulation.
- Imposes sanctions if emotion-based prediction infringes on free decision-making.

Emotion manipulation is now seen not only as a privacy concern but as a direct threat to democracy itself.

United Nations:

In 2021, the UN declared emotions, beliefs, and memories to be essential parts of "inner identity" under the Human-centered AI Principles:

- These cannot be violated.
- Technology must never intervene invisibly.
- Human dignity must always take precedence over technological convenience.

Canada:

Through the Artificial Intelligence and Data Act (AIDA), Canada classified emotion-recognition AI as a high-risk technology in 2022:

- Public-sector use of emotion-reading AI is restricted.

- Emotion-based decision systems require mandatory risk assessment.

Germany:

Germany is moving toward constitutional reforms that treat emotional manipulation not just as a privacy violation, but as a direct violation of personal rights:

- Discussions on banning emotionally manipulative political advertising are underway.
- Mental autonomy (Mentale Autonomie) is now seen as a right requiring constitutional protection.

Emotions Must Be Legally Recognized

Emotions are not just fleeting feelings. They are the foundation of human experience and decision-making. If emotions are shaken, judgment wavers. If judgment wavers, lives unravel. When emotions are unprotected, humanity itself is unprotected.

Even if emotions are not recorded or measured, they are real. Even if emotions are not stored as data, they exist. Emotions are the purest evidence of human existence, something no machine can truly replicate.

Just because technology can measure emotion does not mean it should. Just because it can predict emotional responses does not mean it has the right to manipulate them. Emotion is still, and must always remain, the last sanctuary of human dignity.

Thus, we must first legally declare that emotions "exist." We must recognize emotional flow as something to be protected. Inducing or manipulating emotions without consent must be classified as a rights violation. Emotional data must be treated not as marketing material, but as sacred personal information. Victims of emotional invasion should never again be forced to "prove" their pain. They must be protected first and foremost.

Technology must stop before it reaches emotions. And the law must stand as a barrier that technology cannot cross. Emotion is humanity's deepest freedom—and that freedom must live not only in our hearts, but in our laws.

Chapter 19: Emotions Must Be Protected by the Constitution

This Is a Constitutional Issue

Emotions are not just reactions. Emotions are the starting point of all the philosophy contained in the word "human." Yet now, technology has quietly crossed that boundary. Emotions are being measured in real time, judgments are subtly induced, and memories are treated like reorganizable data. People still believe, "I am who I am." But one day, we find ourselves quietly doubting whether the emotions we feel are truly ours, whether the past we remember really belongs to us. What I feel, why I make certain decisions— we now unknowingly move along pre-designed flows.

This is a constitutional issue. The law exists to protect human dignity. If the most fundamental pillars of human existence—emotion, memory, and judgment—are shaken, that disturbance must be declared within the language of law. Emotions can be measured. But just because they can be measured doesn't mean they should be manipulated. Memories can be organized like files. But when their emotional depth is lost, memories cease to be lived experience and become narratives crafted by others.

The current law protects bodies, property, and speech. But what about emotions? Memories? Consciousness? We now live in a vacuum where "emotions exist but are not protected." If memories and emotions no longer feel like mine, it signals that technology has already outpaced the Constitution. Redefining these boundaries is the law's most urgent promise.

Article 10: Human Dignity and the Right to Happiness
Article 10 of the Constitution of the Republic of Korea states:
"All citizens are entitled to the dignity and worth of the human person and the right to pursue happiness."

This article has long served as the foundation for freedom of expression, protection of privacy, equality, and the right to self-determination. It prevented the government or others from invading an individual's life. But now, we must ask the question at a deeper level: Technology designs the emotions we feel, the judgments we make based on those emotions, and the lives we choose thereafter.

In this era, "happiness" is no longer an abstract idea. Happiness can only exist when emotional flow is truly autonomous. "Dignity" can only survive when emotions remain unmanipulated. Therefore, we must ask again: "Is happiness even possible if my emotions can be manipulated?" If my emotions are measured without consent, quietly adjusted through stimuli, and if my actions and choices are shaped by those altered emotions—am I still freely pursuing happiness?

Emotions shape human judgment. Judgments form human lives. If emotions are shaken, dignity becomes hollow, and happiness becomes manufactured. If I cannot be sure that the emotions I feel are my own, I can no longer take full responsibility for my choices and my life.

Emotional sovereignty is the natural extension of Article 10. Dignity survives when external manipulation is absent. Happiness becomes genuine only when emotional flows are protected. If emotions cannot be safeguarded, neither freedom, nor choices, nor the future truly belong to us.

Why Emotional Rights Must Be Included in the Constitution

Proposal for a Constitutional Amendment: Emotional Rights

"All citizens are entitled to the dignity and worth of the human person and the right to pursue happiness. Emotions, memories, and consciousness, as essential components of human identity, possess the right to autonomy and inviolability. The state has a duty to protect individuals from technologies, information, and algorithms that intrude upon or influence their inner selves and to guarantee that emotions flow and develop autonomously without external interference."

For decades, human rights have focused on the body, expression, property, and equality. But today, emotions must also be protected. Emotional sovereignty naturally follows from Article 10. Emotions must be safeguarded because when emotions falter, judgment wavers, memories distort, and life itself loses stability. The manipulation of emotions silences human dignity.

Emotional Rights would ensure that no external force can measure or manipulate emotional flows without consent. It would defend the deepest structure of selfhood—the ability to experience, feel, and decide freely.

What the World Would Look Like if Emotions Were Constitutionally Protected

If emotional rights were protected, advertising algorithms would need to disclose emotion analysis transparently. Right now, your emotions are secretly predicted, and products are pushed based on the most vulnerable emotional state. With constitutional protection, platforms would need to seek explicit consent before analyzing emotional flows. Secretly exploiting emotional vulnerability for sales would become a recognized rights violation.

Judgment-manipulating technologies would require prior explanation and consent. AI recommendation engines or news feeds would not be allowed to hide emotional manipulation structures. Labels like "This content was curated based on emotional analysis" would become mandatory. If emotional manipulation occurred without consent, companies would bear legal liability for violating constitutional rights.

Victims of emotional invasion would no longer be dismissed with, "It's just your mood."

Today, even when technology shakes our emotions, it is trivialized. But if emotional rights are protected, victims could claim emotional flow manipulation as a constitutional violation. Technology providers would be required to prove they did not engage in emotional manipulation—and be held accountable if they did.

In this new world, emotions would no longer be treated as disposable marketing data. Emotions would be protected as the core of human dignity. Technology may approach emotions, but it would no longer have the unchecked freedom to exploit them.

The Constitution: Humanity's Last Line of Defense

Now that technology has touched the innermost depths of human existence, the final wall of protection must be the Constitution.

Emotions, memories, and consciousness—these are not luxuries. They are the core of what it means to be human. Emotions allow us to meet the world. Memories bridge the past and present. Consciousness allows us to know, "I am me."

Technology is quietly breaching these boundaries. What must humans protect? It is no longer enough to guard the body, property, or even free speech. We must now defend the entire inner self—emotion, memory, and consciousness. The Constitution is humanity's last defense.

Technology will grow even smarter, quieter, and more seamless. It will touch emotions, memories, and decisions without our awareness. To remain human, we need just one clear barrier: "This line cannot be crossed." That line must be declared through the Constitution.

The Constitution preserves the minimal conditions for human dignity. It forbids reckless intrusion into the mind. It affirms that emotions, memories, and consciousness belong to the person alone. No matter how far technology advances, that sentence must remain loyal to humanity.

Reference

Scientific Research & Projects

- DARPA. (n.d.). *Biological Technologies Office*. Defense Advanced Research Projects Agency. Retrieved from https://www.darpa.mil/about-us/offices/bto

- Emotiv. (n.d.). *Brain-computer interfaces and brainwave sensing technology*. Retrieved from https://www.emotiv.com/

- OpenWorm. (n.d.). An open science project to simulate C. elegans. Retrieved from http://www.openworm.org/

- Neuralink. (n.d.). Developing ultra high bandwidth brain-machine interfaces. Retrieved from https://neuralink.com/

- BrainGate Research Consortium. (2006). Neural interface system for individuals with tetraplegia. Nature, 442(7099), 164–171. https://doi.org/10.1038/nature04970

- Kernel. (n.d.). Kernel Flow: Non-invasive brain recording device. Retrieved from https://www.kernel.com/flow

- Neuro-Insight. (n.d.). Measuring real-time brain responses to marketing stimuli. Retrieved from https://www.neuro-insight.com/

Ethical Guidelines and International Regulations

- European Parliament and Council. (2016). Regulation (EU) 2016/679: General Data Protection Regulation (GDPR). Official Journal of the European Union. Retrieved from https://eur-lex.europa.eu/eli/reg/2016/679/oj

- United Nations. (2021). Recommendation on the Ethics of Artificial Intelligence. UNESCO. Retrieved from https://unesdoc.unesco.org/ark:/48223/pf0000380455

- U.S. Senate. (2022). Emotion AI Regulation Act (Draft Legislation). Retrieved from https://www.congress.gov/

- Government of Canada. (2022). Artificial Intelligence and Data Act (AIDA). Retrieved from https://ised-isde.canada.ca/site/innovation-better-canada/en/artificial-intelligence-and-data-act

Notable Events and Case Studies

- NSO Group Technologies. (n.d.). Pegasus spyware and its impact on privacy and surveillance. Multiple journalistic investigations.

- Facebook. (2014). Experimental evidence of massive-scale emotional contagion through social networks. Proceedings of the National Academy of Sciences, 111(24), 8788–8790. https://doi.org/10.1073/pnas.1320040111

- Netflix Tech Blog. (2021). Optimizing show openings with machine learning. Retrieved from

  https://netflixtechblog.com/

- TikTok Transparency Reports. (n.d.). Algorithmic recommendation systems. Retrieved from https://www.tiktok.com/transparency/en/

- Amazon Patents. (2017). Physical and emotional state detection system (U.S. Patent No. 9,847,589). United States Patent and Trademark Office.

- Walmart Patents. (2017). System and method for analyzing emotional states of users in a retail environment (Patent application). United States Patent and Trademark Office.

- Xiaoshan Airport. (2018). *Facial recognition-based emotional detection for airport security*. Hangzhou, China.

Medical Studies

- George, M. S., Lisanby, S. H., & Sackeim, H. A. (1999). Transcranial magnetic stimulation: Applications in neuropsychiatry. Archives of General Psychiatry, 56(4), 300–311. https://doi.org/10.1001/archpsyc.56.4.300
- Nitsche, M. A., & Paulus, W. (2000). Excitability changes induced in the human motor cortex by weak transcranial direct current stimulation. The Journal of Physiology, 527(3), 633–639. https://doi.org/10.1111/j.1469-7793.2000.t01-1-00633.x
- Mayberg, H. S., Lozano, A. M., Voon, V., et al. (2005). Deep brain stimulation for treatment-resistant depression. Neuron, 45(5), 651–660. https://doi.org/10.1016/j.neuron.2005.02.014
- Kühn, A. A., & Volkmann, J. (2017). Innovative technology for brain modulation in neuropsychiatric disorders: Deep brain stimulation and beyond. Current

Opinion in Neurology, 30(5), 473–480.
https://doi.org/10.1097/WCO.0000000000000488